Improving Concentration

D1333670

ISBN–13: 978-1-902523-63-6
ISBN–10: 1-902523-63-6

Author: Ian Maynard
Editor: Penny Crisfield
Sub-editors: Chris Harwood, Chris Sellars and Chris Shambrook
Typesetter: Lisa Furness
Cover photo courtesy of actionplus sports images

Published on behalf of
sports coach UK by

Coachwise Business Solutions

sports coach UK
114 Cardigan Road
Headingley
Leeds LS6 3BJ
Tel: 0113-274 4802 Fax: 0113-275 5019
Email: coaching@sportscoachuk.org
Website: www.sportscoachuk.org

Patron: HRH The Princess Royal

Coachwise Business Solutions
Coachwise Ltd
Chelsea Close
Off Amberley Road
Armley
Leeds LS12 4HP
Tel: 0113-231 1310 Fax: 0113-231 9606
Email: enquiries@coachwisesolutions.co.uk
Website: www.coachwisesolutions.co.uk

sports coach UK will ensure that it has professional and ethical values and that all its practices are inclusive and equitable.

050480

Preface

Many factors contribute to sports performance. In addition to the physical, technical and strategic demands of sport, performers must be able to remain focused, maintain emotional control, sustain self-confidence and constantly apply themselves in both training and competition. In your own sport, you will undoubtedly be able to recognise the mental demands placed on performers. Meeting these demands may be relatively easy when things are going well but less so during times of difficulty – for example when form is poor, there are distractions or an injury is sustained. Coaches typically identify a range of mental qualities that seem to underpin successful sports performance – qualities largely encompassed in the four Cs: commitment, confidence, concentration and control.

Few participants involved in sport would disagree with the notion that the ability to gain and maintain focus or concentrate effectively is one of the mental keys to successful performance. This exciting booklet will help coaches and performers understand and improve concentration. It includes a wealth of ideas that can be readily integrated into everyday coaching practice without making substantial changes to existing sessions and programmes. It provides a model of attentional style outlining how different individuals may concentrate, how concentration demands may vary across sports and identifies the common problems associated with concentration in sport. A series of techniques and strategies are provided to help develop and maintain appropriate concentration.

The booklet is divided into two parts:

Part One, written in home study format, contains three chapters. It provides an overview of mental skills training, an introduction to understanding and improving concentration and guidance on the importance of performance profiling in assessing performer needs. These chapters will help you to:

- identify the contribution of the fundamental mental skills to overall sports performance
- assess your knowledge of basic mental skills training methods
- explain the importance of concentration to performance in your sport
- profile performers to identify their strengths and weaknesses.

Part Two consists of eight practical mental skill programmes – many involve working directly with your performer/s either within or outside your normal coaching sessions. These practical sessions will help you to understand and improve concentration through identifying the most important training and competition cues for your sport and your performers; controlling high arousal; using process goals, routines, imagery and performance planning; and integrating a range of mental skills into a concentration training package. By working through the programmes with your performers, you should be able to identify:

- ways that mental skills can improve concentration
- how mental skills training can be incorporated into your overall training programmes
- a strategy (action plan) to ensure your performers can develop and maintain their concentration.

A final summary with follow-up references concludes the booklet.

This is an essential booklet for coaches and performers looking for the winning edge – it may also be of benefit to sport psychologists, team managers and support staff.

Key to symbols used in the text:

 An activity.

 Approximate length of time to be spent on the activity.

Contents

Contents

Chapter One: Overview of Mental Skills Training

1.0   What's in It for You?

The field of mental skills training is still relatively new to many coaches, although the importance of the mind in sport has been recognised for many years. Sport involves a mind game as well as a physical performance and without developing qualities such as confidence, commitment, concentration and control, peak performance will remain an unattainable dream for most performers.

Before examining concentration in more detail, it is helpful to consider the effect of mental factors on sports performance and help you assess your experience and knowledge in the use of mental training skills. This chapter provides an overview and by the end, you should be able to:

- identify the contribution of the fundamental qualities (the 4Cs) to overall performance in your sport
- assess your knowledge and experience of basic mental skills training methods
- communicate to your performers the value of mental practice to improve their sports performance.

1.1   Importance of Mental Qualities

You are probably already aware of the influence of mental factors on sports performance – in learning new skills as well as in producing consistent high level performance. How often is a competition won by the performer who:

- handles pressure better
- is totally committed to a tough training regime
- maintains concentration in spite of distractions
- remains confident in spite of setbacks?

The first activity will help you to consider the impact of mental factors on your performers.

ACTIVITY I

1   Reflect on a recent coaching session or competition in which one of your performers:

- performed well beyond expectation
- significantly under-performed.

2   List all the reasons why you felt the performer over- or under-achieved:

Over-achieved	Under-achieved

You may find you have listed some reasons that are directly concerned with the performer's mental state (eg lacked self-confidence, frustrated by weather conditions, anger at official's decisions, inspired by the crowd). Alternatively you may find some of the reasons are essentially physical, technical or tactical (eg skills broke down under the opposition's pressure).

To what extent might these reasons result in changes in mental state? (eg Did the fear of repeated injury influence self-confidence? Was the performer's focus too much on the opposition rather than his/her own performance?)

3   To what extent did the outcome influence the performer's:

- assessment of performance?   not at all/somewhat/a great deal
- subsequent mental state or approach
  to training and competition?   not at all/somewhat/a great deal

List any mental factors you believe might have contributed to the over- or under-achievement or subsequent mental state:

-

-

-

4 Identify the key situations in your sport when these factors might be important (eg at the start, at a penalty, following an injury):

-

-

-

Now turn over.

2   *Some of the reasons listed to explain over-achievement and under-achievement might have included:*

Reasons for over-achieving	Reasons for under-achieving
Retention of agreed game plan	Lack of fitness
Good mental and physical preparation	Poor weather conditions or facilities
Maintenance of focus and emotional control	Unfavourable officiating decisions
Selection of appropriate equipment (eg club, racing tyres)	Injury or fear of injury
Ideal conditions (eg no wind, dry pitch)	Strength of opponent
Ability to adapt to changing circumstances (eg score line, opponent's tactics)	Breakdown in skills
	Poor tactical decisions
	Failure to cope with pressure – choked at a critical point
High confidence due to good fitness level.	Distraction (eg from crowd, officials, opponent, incident)
	Failure by other team members.

3   *The sort of mental factors you may have listed could probably be summarised under the 4Cs:*

- *Commitment (ie will to win, toughness).*
- *Control of emotions (eg of anxiety, anger, frustration).*
- *Concentration (ie focus).*
- *Confidence (ie positive attitude, self-belief).*

4   *Consider your answers by reviewing the following specific situations that in some sports might make significant demands on mental qualities:*

- *At the start of a race, game or event.*
- *The end of a race, last ten minutes of a game, final event (eg last jump, last piece of apparatus).*
- *Following a foul, an unfavourable officiating decision, an injury, equipment failure.*
- *Before a difficult or particularly crucial situation (eg the jump following a no-jump, the most difficult piece of apparatus, at a penalty, in extra time, at a scrum close to your own try line).*

You will probably have recognised that mental factors contribute significantly to performance in your sport[1]. To illustrate the potential significance of mental qualities, read the following example from tennis.

Sampras versus Moya, Australian Open 1997

Total play time: 87 minutes

Action time: 17 minutes

Time between action: 70 minutes (potential thinking time)

During these 70 minutes, there was the opportunity for both negative and positive thoughts, feelings and self-talk; plenty of time to think oneself into or out of the match.

1.2 Mental Training Techniques

Most competitors use a variety of mental techniques – often as a result of experience or trial and error rather than through teaching. They have learnt strategies to help them cope with difficult situations both in a sports context and perhaps in life more generally (eg dealing with examinations, interviews, work pressures, relationships). Coaches can accelerate and enhance this process by introducing and systematically developing appropriate techniques for specific occasions. You may already use or be familiar with a number of techniques. Try Activity 2.

---

1   If you need further guidance in identifying the contribution of mental factors to your sport, you are recommended to read **Mental Skills: An Introduction for Sports Coaches**, available from Coachwise 1st4sport (0113-201 5555).

ACTIVITY 2

1   List any mental skills you or your performers use (with or without your
    input) or may wish to use to improve the mental qualities listed in the left-
    hand column. An example skill for each quality is given to help you:

Qualities	Skills
Commitment	*Goal-setting*
Concentration	*Imagery*
Control	*Relaxation training*
Confidence	*Positive self-talk/statements*

2   Describe in more detail the skills you have listed under **concentration:**

Now turn over.

1   *The following table provides an overview of the type of skills that can be used to strengthen each quality:*

Qualities	Skills
Commitment	Goal-setting Refocusing Positive thinking (eg use of positive statements)
Concentration	Imagery Distraction training Developing routines and using crib cards Performance planning Identifying performance cues Relaxation training Simulated competition training
Control	Relaxation training Breathing exercises (eg centring) Cognitive restructuring Positive self-statements Developing routines Simulated competition training
Confidence	Positive self-talk/statements Imagery Goal-setting Routines Cognitive restructuring (positive thinking) Simulated competition training

2   *The skills listed under* **concentration** *will be the focus of subsequent sessions in this pack. You should note that many of the skills in this category also appear elsewhere. This demonstrates the versatility of these skills and the way in which they can be integrated into an overall mental skills strategy.*

If you had any difficulty with this activity or if any of the techniques are new to you, you may find it useful to develop your understanding further before continuing with this pack. You are recommended to look at the **sports coach UK** home study pack: **Mental Skills: An Introduction for Sports Coaches**, as well as other mental skills packs (available from Coachwise 1st4sport, 0113-201 5555).

1.3   Learning Mental Skills

Whatever skills (mental, technical, physical) you wish your performers to develop, the cyclical process through which they learn, practise and apply the skills remains much the same:

Step 1

Identify all the factors (or qualities) that can positively affect performance. You may wish to profile your performer's qualities separately in each of the following areas or take a whole performer approach (ie profile your performer's strengths and weaknesses on those qualities deemed most important): technical, tactical, physical, mental.

Step 2

Identify with each performer, his or her strengths and weaknesses in relation to each quality. This profiling can be recorded using the performance profiling techniques introduced in Section 3.1 (page 64).

Step 3

From this profiling, you will be able to determine with each performer the key qualities that will result in the most profound improvements in performance. For example, the key factor might be improved concentration, greater power, better decision-making.

Step 4

Select the most appropriate way to make this improvement – you need to know the range of techniques possible and how to use them effectively.

Step 5

Determine when the technique should be introduced into training, practice and eventually competition (see Section 1.4). For some mental techniques (eg imagery), there is also the question of when the technique can be used (eg before, during and after the session or competition).

Step 6

Practise the technique – probably first in training and mock competitions. After a suitable period of time, monitor and assess the effectiveness of the technique. This can involve re-profiling your performer to check for relative improvements. If necessary, the performer may persist with this technique or use an alternative from the range available.

Step 7

Application of the skill in actual competition – this should be done gradually and monitored carefully; start in less important competitions and progress to the more important ones.

NB   Mental skills, like physical skills, take time to learn, practise and use successfully – be patient and build them slowly.

While many performers might recognise the impact of improved technical skills and fitness on sport success, some may be more reluctant to acknowledge the need to commit time and effort to the development of mental qualities. You may need therefore to discuss the potential value of mental skills training with your performers, so they appreciate what you are trying to achieve and how it will improve performance. This enhanced sense of ownership will increase their commitment and adherence to mental training. How and when you do this will depend very much on the performer – his or her profile, expectations, goals and training programme.

At what point in the training and competition calendar should you start to introduce new mental skills? This will depend on a number of factors such as the following:

- Your performers' needs and goals, the relative importance of mental skills work to other aspects of training and their current use of mental skills.

- The stage in the training cycle – new mental skills should normally be introduced in the off-season, pre or early phase of the annual programme – not when they are undergoing new or particularly heavy training loads or in the major competition phase.

- Your availability of time – it is best to introduce new mental skills when you have time to talk these through thoroughly with your performers.

ACTIVITY 3

1 Determine when you intend to introduce new mental skills into the training programme for your performer. NB It may be helpful now to select one or two performers with whom you might work as you read through this pack.

Mark these points on the chart provided.

Jan	Feb	Mar	Apr	May	Jun	Jul	Aug	Sept	Oct	Nov	Dec

2 Explain your decision:

1.4 Significance of Concentration

The significance of concentration to successful sporting performance will probably have become clear by now. Outcomes in sport are very often decided by a small margin which in many cases can be traced back to a lapse in concentration.

> *It is hard to imagine a variable more central to performance than the ability to direct and control one's concentration.*

> *Nideffer, 1976*

However, what exactly is concentration? Why is it sometimes so easy to focus on the game, yet on other occasions your mind focuses on anything other than the game? How can you deal with lapses in concentration? These are the sorts of questions asked by both coaches and performers seeking peak and consistent performance.

ACTIVITY 4

1   Explain what concentration means to you:

2   Reflect on an occasion when you or your performer experienced good concentration and describe what you noticed (eg feelings, thoughts, attention focus):

Occasion (eg a particular competition):

I noticed (eg feeling of calm):

---

3   Reflect on an occasion when you or your performer experienced poor concentration and describe what you noticed (eg feelings, thoughts, attention focus):

Occasion (eg a particular competition):

I noticed (eg worry about the outcome):

4   Describe in as much detail as possible the effects of differing levels of concentration on performance:

Good Concentration	Poor Concentration

Now turn over.

1 Concentration is a limited resource – there is only a certain amount available so it is important it is directed at the most important factors and not at irrelevant distractions. In sport, this means focusing on relevant cues (eg the ball in tennis or golf, the stroke rate in swimming) and not on uncontrollable external factors such as the weather or internal distractions such as worrying about losing. The ability to sustain concentration on the right cues seems to underpin consistent performance. It is a skill – to minimise distractions and maximise attention on relevant or critical cues. It can be improved with practice but is not, however, about trying harder – many people argue concentration is best in a more relaxed state, sometimes described as being in the zone.

2/3 The following table describes experiences often associated with good and poor concentration in tennis. Compare it with your answers:

	Good Concentration	Poor Concentration
Thoughts	Positive Challenged My game is flowing	Negative – what if I lose? Overloaded with information, poor decision-making Easily distracted
Feelings	Calm Control Sense of anticipation Enjoyment without effort	Tense, heavy Tired Everything requires a great deal of effort Lack of motivation
Focus	Task at hand – the here and now (performance goals) **During the point:** looking for the seam on the ball, opponent's movements/racket **Between points:** the next point	**Ahead:** eventual score/outcome **Back:** mistakes, bad line calls **During the point:** task irrelevant factors (eg the weather/score) **Between points:** task irrelevant factors (eg the last error, spectators)

4   *It is important to remember that concentration is unique to the individual. How can you tell when you or your performer are well focused? Perhaps the descriptors in the previous table could be used as prompts to ask your performers about their concentration (eg Do you manage to stay in the here and now during a competition? Do you feel tense or calm? What are the distractions that interfere with concentration? Are they external or internal (inside your head)?).*

The preceding table is simplistic but provides an overview of some of the common experiences associated with concentration. All are generalisations – each performer's reaction is unique (and can be very different from others). Therefore it is important to talk specifically to your performer/s about their thoughts and feelings; why they are concentrating well and when they are distracted.

1.5   Summary and Further Help

In this chapter, you have been encouraged to reflect on the significance of mental qualities (especially concentration) to success in sport and the potential of mental skills training techniques. In the next chapter, the techniques that can best be used to improve concentration will be considered in more detail. In Chapter Three, the importance of mental skills work to your performers will be reviewed and you will be encouraged to profile your performer's strengths and weaknesses. You will then be able to work through the programmes in Part Two in the order that best suits your needs and those of your performers.

If the area of mental skills training is fairly new to you, you may find the following packs helpful (available from Coachwise 1st4sport, 0113-201 5555):

sports coach UK (2001) **Physiology and Performance**. 3rd edition
Leeds: Coachwise Solutions/The National Coaching Foundation. ISBN 0-947850-24-4

Sellars, C. (2004) **Mental Skills: An Introduction for Sports Coaches**.
Leeds: Coachwise Solutions/The National Coaching Foundation. ISBN 0-947850-34-1.

Chapter Two: Introduction to Concentration

2.0   What's in It for You?

> *The secret of concentration is not to let outside factors register. Be aware of them but keep them outside the bubble in which you are operating.*
>
> *Geoff Boycott*

The most successful performers appear to have the ability to focus on the relevant cues in their environment and sustain that focus for the desired period of time. Probably the most important aspect of concentration to consider at this stage is that it is a psychological skill that can be learned and developed through practice and dedication.

Coaches can play a large part in improving a performer's concentration. Good coaches do this in a number of ways – for example, by the way they:

- focus and build on a performer's strengths

- encourage performers to recognise optimal arousal states (ideal performance states, IPS)

- establish performance routines

- provide positive reinforcement, encouragement and reassurance

- build a performance plan which progressively builds on each success towards the ultimate goals

- encourage and empower performers to accept responsibility for their own actions and help them develop the skills to gain the mental toughness to cope effectively in any situation.

The way coaches develop programmes and interact with their performers is considered in many other books. This pack focuses primarily on the last point – on helping performers learn a range of mental training techniques to help them improve concentration. A number of skills are described: identifying performance cues, reducing anxiety, controlling the controllable factors, developing routines, using imagery and simulated training[1].

---

1   For further help on the mental training techniques, refer to the summary section of this chapter or request a Coachwise 1st4sport catalogue (0113-201 5555) for an up-to-date listing of new packs.

Each skill will be considered in this chapter to help you:

- explore how it works
- identify the benefits and disadvantages
- assess its relative merits in meeting your needs and those of your performers
- evaluate when and why to use it, and how it can be integrated into regular training programmes and competition.

Like most qualities associated with sports performance, concentration can be improved using various training techniques. That's the good news – however, to be effective, these techniques must be learned, practised, used regularly and integrated into other aspects of performance preparation and competition. As you read, it is important to remember that each mental skill will be best developed by adhering to the learning principles described in Section 1.3 (page 9).

This chapter provides an understanding of the concept of concentration and a rationale for selecting and implementing the mental skills programmes in Part Two, so it is important to work through it carefully[1].

2.1 Concentration in Sport

Concentration is about focusing all your attention on those things which are relevant to whatever it is you are doing. It is universally agreed that to achieve in sport, performers need good concentration skills but good concentration is not about trying harder – in fact, peak performances are often accompanied by a state of relaxed or effortless concentration. Where should their concentration be focused? Which cues are relevant at any particular time? Although every sport has unique cues, there are some common denominators and it is helpful to analyse the attentional demands of a sport by considering a model (Nideffer, 1976) depicting two dimensions:

- The **width** of attention – whether attention is broad or narrow, the number of cues to which the performer should attend. A very broad focus of attention may be desirable for certain sport skills, such as when a midfield player in soccer or hockey is reading the opposition defence to try to find openings to make a good penetrating pass. A narrower focus is preferred when taking a penalty or when hitting a cricket, golf or tennis ball because it forces concentration on a limited number of important cues.

---

1   If the information is new to you, you may find it useful to read through the **sports coach UK** home study pack, **Mental Skills: An Introduction for Sports Coaches,** available from Coachwise 1st4sport (0113-201 5555).

- The **direction** of attention – whether attention is directed outwards on the events happening in the external environment or internally – focused on the performer's thoughts and feelings. An external focus is frequently needed to concentrate on the position or movement of other performers, an external object such as the ball or piece of equipment or to weigh up the weather conditions before releasing an arrow in archery. An internal focus is preferred when there is a need to analyse what is happening, plan strategy or rehearse a movement (eg using imagery before a free throw in basketball).

To analyse the attentional demands of any skill or activity in sports, you need to consider both of these dimensions together. Some examples of the four different types of attentional focus in sport are shown in Figure 1.

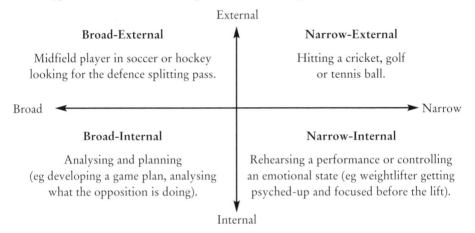

Figure 1: Nideffer's (1976) two-dimensional model for understanding the attentional demands of sport with examples

The ability to gain the right attentional focus is crucial and so too is the ability to switch from one type of attention to another. Some sports make greater demands on certain types of attentional focus and more critically on the need to switch frequently and quickly from one to another. The skill in creating and maintaining a particular focus and indeed of switching effortlessly varies from one performer to another. The next activity will help you to consider when each might be important in your sport.

ACTIVITY 5

1   Consider the attentional demands of your sport and try to jot down examples in each of the four quadrants of when it would be appropriate to adopt each style:

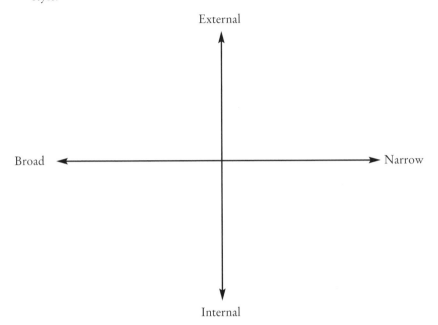

External

Broad ←――――――――――――――――――――――→ Narrow

Internal

2   Analyse the importance of each and the need for flexibility to switch from one to another:

Now turn over.

1   *Use the following example from basketball to help you assess your analysis matrix:*

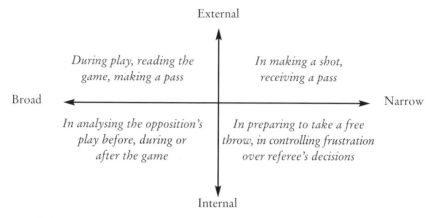

2   *All four are important at different times in preparing, playing and analysing the game so the need to be able to switch effectively from one to another is an important skill for basketball players.*

Not only do sports vary in the attentional focus and flexibility each demands, they also may vary in the length of time the concentration needs to be maintained. Some demand continuous concentration (eg motor racing) while in others it can be more intermittent (eg golf), although some players prefer to maintain concentration rather than repeatedly refocus. The duration of the event should also be considered – the short duration of sprint events or a gymnastics vault compared with the length of a marathon or five set tennis match. It may therefore be helpful to generate a second two-dimensional matrix (Figure 2). The examples provided may help you locate your sport on the concentration continuum.

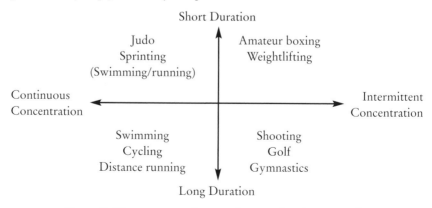

Figure 2: The concentration continuum showing examples

The concentration continuum highlights not only the need for a performance focus but also (especially in intermittent sports) the ability to refocus. In sports where the performer can largely control when to execute the skill (in self-paced skills such as the golf swing, tennis serve), there is a ready opportunity to refocus prior to execution.

Attentional problems

As well as understanding how individuals may differ in their concentration style and how sports may differ in their concentration demands, it is also useful to understand the different types of concentration problems that may occur in sport. These concentration problems are usually caused by an inappropriate attentional focus or what might be referred to as a **distraction**. Instead of focusing on the relevant cues at a given point in the competition, the performer becomes distracted by other events, thoughts or emotions. Anything which is irrelevant to the task in hand is a potential distraction. In accordance with Nideffer's direction dimension, distractions can be external (in the environment – weather, spectators, officials) or internal (task irrelevant thoughts – dwelling on past mistakes or decisions, worrying about the outcome and its repercussions). Study the following table and then use the next activity to analyse the typical distractions that characterise your sport or a particular performer you coach.

External Distractions	Internal Distractions
Background noise	Thinking about other competitions
Players talking at inappropriate times	Attending to past events like a recent mistake
Aeroplanes/trains	Attending to future events like 'what if I lose this match?'
Action on an adjacent table, position, court or pitch or in the spectator area	Thinking too much (eg body stroke execution)
Noticing family and friends in the audience	Mental rehearsal at inappropriate times

ACTIVITY 6

List examples of external and internal distractions you or your performers have experienced:

External Distractions	Internal Distractions

Take a closer look at a few of the typical problems that sportspeople have in attempting to maintain concentration. As you read through, think about occasions when you or one or your performers have experienced each concentration problem.

Attending to too many cues. One of the difficult aspects of participating in any level of sport is that there are many distractions in the environment that compete for your attentional focus. Performers who tend to favour a broad-external attentional strength are particularly troubled by other things going on around them; they seem to notice everything that is happening in their immediate vicinity, much of which is irrelevant to their performance (at that time) – for example the equipment used by the opposition, who is watching the competition or who the coach is talking to on the sideline. The list of potential distractions is endless and because performers have little control over most of these factors, it becomes all the more imperative to cope effectively through proper concentration skills.

NB Performers need to learn to focus on the appropriate relevant cue/s.

Attending to past events. A concentration problem that plagues many sportspeople is their inability to forget about what happened previously, either during this competition or even previous competitions. The inappropriate internal focus on past events has been the downfall of many talented players. The tennis player who cannot forget the double fault served at set point, the gymnast still troubled by a poor score in the preceding routine, the team player incensed by another player's error resulting in conceding a goal, an official's unfavourable decision at a critical point in the match – they all create an internal distraction which prevents the performer refocusing on the here and now, on the current situation, with a consequential negative effect on performance.

NB Performers need to develop skills that help them to stay calm, evaluate the options to limit the damage, put the negative thoughts behind them and stay focused in the present on the task relevant cues.

Attending to future events. It is all too easy, particularly for young or inexperienced performers, for thoughts to slip into the future and focus on the future consequences of certain actions – What if I get/lose a big lead? What if I win/lose this race? What these statements have in common is their **irrelevance** to the here and now and the relevant cues. Worrying about what might happen acts purely as a distraction and causes excess anxiety, muscle tension and/or tentative performance.

NB It is important to stay in the present and/or very near future.

Paralysis by analysis. Another type of inappropriate attentional focus that can lead to performance problems, is focusing internally for too long. It is important to understand when an internal focus is beneficial and when it is detrimental to performance. By getting stuck inside your head, you are no longer attending to the important cues from the environment, so problems can occur. For instance, when refining your body position in a gymnastic tumble, it is important to focus your attention internally to get the kinaesthetic feel of your body position. However, this kind of analysis, often accompanied by a string of self-instructions, may at times be helpful in training but only until the refinement is automatic. Problems will arise if this type of internal-narrow thinking takes place for too long during competitive performance.

NB A useful guideline in many sports is to spend the majority of the time in training thinking about performance but the majority of time in competition just doing it (especially the more open sports).

A number of other conditions such as anxiety and fatigue have an impact on concentration.

Impact of anxiety

One of the frequent causes of poor concentration is anxiety. Under normal conditions, attention is continually shifting back and forth across the four different types of attentional style. Increasing pressure and the accompanying anxiety and worrying interferes not only with physical performance but also with the ability to maintain good mental flexibility. Under pressure, three things happen to your attention or concentration:

1   **Attentional inflexibility.** Even before you are aware that you are pressured, you begin to rely more heavily on your own particular attentional strength. This is usually the quadrant in which you feel most comfortable – sometimes the quadrant you feel has brought your previous best performance (unfortunately this may not be the appropriate attentional style to use). This reduces flexibility because you are less likely to shift attention in response to changing environmental demands and consequently incompatibility develops between the demand of the task and attentional style. Figure 3 illustrates the strengths and weaknesses of each of the four attentional styles.

External

Strength: reads a complex environment well (eg find the defence splitting pass).

Weakness: may react too quickly without thinking (eg keep selecting the wrong option).

Strength: good concentration on one thing (eg the ball during a rally).

Weakness: may stick to the same response even though it is not working (eg in sailing, going left up the beat, when the right is consistently paying).

Broad ⟵   ⟶ Narrow

Strength: good analytical ability, organises and makes long-range plans (eg through post-match analysis).

Weakness: can become overly analytical, have trouble sticking to one thing. May not react quickly enough (eg thinking when you should be doing).

Strength: good concentration on one thought or idea (eg knowing what you have to achieve in the last activity of a series).

Weakness: fails to attend to and incorporate new information; not sensitive to what is going on around (eg misses the unmarked player in a good scoring position).

Internal

Figure 3: Strengths and weaknesses of each attentional style

2   **Attentional narrowing.** As pressure mounts, attention begins to narrow and it becomes difficult to attend to several things at the same time, resulting in poor decision-making and feeling rushed and overloaded. This is often experienced or described as tunnel vision when it is inappropriate to the sport.

3   **Attention becomes more internally focused.** This occurs as the symptoms of anxiety (increased heart rate, lump in throat, upset stomach, worries) develop. Performers become less attentive to the external task-relevant cues and mistakes increase because the focus often becomes the symptoms of anxiety.

As more performance errors occur, performers tend to become more anxious and tense and so the downward spiral of performance begins. Remember also that good concentration is not about trying harder – it is about relaxed and effortless concentration.

Impact of fatigue

Typically more mistakes are made near the end of a match or competition – often the most vital stage – as a result of tiredness. It takes effort to maintain concentration and as fatigue sets in, concentration wanders and more mistakes are made.

Increased levels of fitness will therefore improve concentration. It may also help to ensure your performers train or practise under the pressure of fatigue to help them cope better in similar situations in competition. Whereas usually coaches ask players to do fitness work at the end of training sessions so fatigue has a minimal effect on skilled performance, occasionally it may be appropriate to do fitness work early in the session so performers become conditioned to maintaining concentration and form when tired.

If the problem areas are discovered (ie problems with ability to shift between the different attentional styles, with decision-making, with anxiety), it is possible to help the performer regain control. The process is similar to analysing a biomechanical problem – once it is known where the error is occurring, it is possible to intervene with specific self-control procedures to rectify the problem area.

ACTIVITY 7

Identify situations in training or competition when distractions occur and describe the problems that result. Two examples are provided to help you. To gain the greatest effect, you may wish to discuss this with a performer to discover his/her particular problem(s), so the most appropriate solution can be implemented:

Situation in which Distraction Occurred	Type of Problem Resulting
Start of important race	*Attending to too many cues (not task relevant)*
During breaks in action (eg dead ball situations, injury stops) or when away from the action in the match	*Thinking of future events (eg tonight's activity, the result, school examinations)*

You will probably find that some performers are better able to concentrate than others and some are more easily distracted than others. Remember each will also experience different problems and you may need to devise a different concentration training programme to solve the difficulty and ultimately improve performance for each performer.

In the next sub-sections, various techniques and strategies will be outlined that have helped coaches and performers in the past to improve concentration:

- Identifying key concentration cues.
- Reducing and controlling anxiety.
- Controlling the controllable factors and maintaining a process orientation – not getting hung up over outcome goals such as winning but focusing on process goals, things that can be achieved now.
- Developing routines to help gain or regain focus – particularly prior to the competition, at crucial times and re-starts.
- Using imagery to facilitate concentration.
- Coping with distractions.

You need to become familiar with each of these so you can select the skill that seems most appropriate to you, your sport and each performer. The way each technique can be introduced and developed will be more fully developed in Part Two of this pack.

2.2   Concentration Cues

One of the most useful techniques for helping coaches and performers improve concentration and focus on the right things at the right time is to make use of concentration cues. This requires identifying the important performance cues or triggers that are central to the execution of the task. These are sometimes referred to as the *fundamental focus* for they ensure a task relevant focus in training or competition from the outset and help refocusing if distractions are experienced. These cues may be words, sights or actions, and may serve a number of functions. Look at the following examples and then try the next activity.

Function	Verbal Cue	Visual Cue	Action Cue
Instructional	Drive from the blocks (athletics/ swimming)	Watch the tell tails on the sails (sailing)	Get your weight forward on your toes before receiving serve (tennis)
Motivational	Go for it, just do it	Seeing yourself on the winning podium at an appropriate time in training	Slapping your thighs, pulling up your socks, putting in your gum shield
Emotional	Relax, calm	The cool, calm collected coach displaying positive signals	Three deep breaths
Psychological	Think broad, here and now	Look for the dot on the ball (squash) or the seam (cricket/tennis)	Squeeze the bat, racket, tiller

Not only do they help to focus attention onto the relevant aspects of the performance, they also help to block out distractions – both internal ones (such as negative thoughts, dwelling on errors) and external ones (such as the crowd, other competitors, the sun).

Fatima Whitbread, the famous javelin thrower, says she deliberately adopts tunnel vision to avoid the distractions of the crowd.

ACTIVITY 8

Select three situations in your sport (at least one in training and one in competition) and identify the appropriate attentional focus:

Training/Competition Situation	Fundamental Focus

Now turn over.

This is not a definitive list but the examples may trigger further examples for you:

Sport	Training/Competition Situation	Fundamental Focus
Sailing	Developing speed during training or competition	Waves Bow tell tails Jib luff Feel of the boat Angle of the boat relative to others.
Rugby	Side-on tackle	Hips of the ball carrier Head behind backside Powerful hit with your shoulder on player's thigh Lock with the arms.
Athletics	100m sprint in competition	**Pre-start:** ready, alert, energised. **Start:** explode, drive, first ten strides, low, power boom. **Middle of race:** pump, smooth. **Finish:** lunge, dip, through the tape.

NB Over time coaches need to help performers identify as many of the
    fundamental foci as possible. However, this should be a gradual process, so
    keep the cues as few and simple as possible.

In some sports or activities, it is relatively easy to identify a few cues that will be more or less your whole game plan. For example, the javelin thrower may make use of three key words to focus attention – focus, accelerate, snap (see Programme Five, page 97 on routines for more details). However, in more open type sports and activities (eg soccer or hockey games) where lots of variables may influence performance (many of which will be outside the performer's control), the coach and performer may be advised to establish well learnt focusing and refocusing routines, and identify critical moments in their sport when a specific concentration cue would be appropriate. Similarly it may also be possible to identify more general concentration cues that often reflect the sport's principles of play. For example in the invasion games (such as soccer, hockey, lacrosse, netball, rugby and basketball) when your team is in possession of the ball, the cue may be support or create space; when not in possession, it might be pressure the opposition or deny space.

ACTIVITY 9

Identify times in your sport when a concentration cue may be appropriate. These may be very specific occasions (eg at a penalty, set play, immediately before action) or more general (eg whenever the opposition has the ball, whenever you are running or cycling immediately behind an opponent):

Specific Situation	General Situation

Some examples are provided in the following panel:

Sport	Specific Situation	General Situation
Soccer	Penalty kick	When opposition has ball
Table tennis	Own serve	Stay close to the table
Athletics	On his/her elbow	Flow
Pistol shooting	Squeeze	Rhythm
Volleyball	Decoys	Communication
Cricket	Bowler's hand	This ball
Gymnastics	Height	Artistry
Swimming	High elbow	Relax

Through experience or practising and playing your sport, you learn what to attend to naturally. However, the speed of learning and level of skill reached can be influenced considerably by a good coach who can read the game accurately and identify where attention should be placed. The coach can then tell performers what to look for in a specific situation. This can be done verbally (via feedback) in practice/simulation type situations, or for other sports, it may be more appropriate to identify these cues away from the usual coaching situation.

Once specific or general situations have been identified when some form of concentration cue may be relevant, you need to establish if performers need instructional, motivational, emotional or psychological cues, and whether they prefer verbal, visual or physical cues. You will have an opportunity to look at how concentration cues are identified and personalised in Programme Two (page 84).

2.3 Reducing and Controlling Anxiety

There is an important and dynamic relationship between many of the mental skills. In particular, the inability of a performer to control excess anxiety (often referred to as choking) will invariably lead to some form of dysfunction in concentration. Remember, however, that pressure itself is not necessarily a negative experience – the rush of adrenaline generated by competition creates certain body symptoms such as sweaty palms, racing heartbeat, muscle tension or butterflies. These are merely the body's way of preparing for competition, for developing the right arousal level known as the *ideal performance state* (IPS).

If the individual is uncertain about what is expected, concerned about his or her ability to meet the demands or where the outcome is especially significant or important, these symptoms of arousal may be interpreted as anxiety or worry rather than readiness.

ACTIVITY 10

Jot down the physical (somatic) or mental (cognitive) feelings you commonly experience before taking part in a sports competition (from the perspective of you as athlete or you as coach). Against each, suggest whether the symptom has a positive or negative effect on subsequent performance (if it is sometimes negative and sometimes positive, place a tick against each column). An example is provided to help you:

	Symptom	Positive Effect	Negative Effect
Physical	*Nausea/butterflies in the stomach*	✔	✔
Mental	*What am I doing here – I'm out of my depth*		✔

Now turn over.

You will no doubt have identified a number of symptoms:

- *Physical ones such as stomach upsets, shaking, sickness, yawning, increased sweating, racing heart rate.*
- *Mental ones such as worry, short temper, aggression and the inability to concentrate.*

Anxiety will initially cause a regression to the preferred attentional strength of the performer (which may not be appropriate for subsequent performance). In addition, high anxiety causes the attentional field to:

- narrow (often referred to as tunnel vision) which usually results in missing task-relevant cues
- become internal – the performer focuses on thoughts (usually negative) which further reduces attention on the vital performance cues.

It should be apparent therefore that one way to improve concentration is to use techniques to limit the perception of anxiety or learn to control it[1]. In addition to teaching anxiety control techniques, coaches can also do a number of things to limit the likelihood of anxiety developing as well:

Step 1: Recognise that high arousal can be a friend as well as an enemy

Performers may perceive some forms of high arousal as a positive prepared state; however, most of the time, many of the aspects of physical and mental anxiety will tend to be construed as a negative experience. Therefore, perhaps an important first step for the coach may be to foster and reinforce the belief that arousal is the body's way of preparing for action, and as such is a necessary way of signalling the performer's readiness to compete. Coaches should talk to performers to find out exactly how they interpret and deal with high arousal states. The answers to these questions will give you insight into not only whether there is a need to teach relaxation skills but it may also indicate if you need to focus on reducing physical (somatic) anxiety, mental (cognitive) anxiety or perhaps both.

Step 2: Control the environment

What aspects of the environment increase the likelihood of athletes experiencing stress and what can you, as a coach, do to change both the physical and social environment? The two big causes of anxiety (especially in young performers) are the:

- uncertainty about whether or not they will be able to do what is expected of them
- perception of the importance of the outcome.

---

1   Anxiety control techniques are considered in greater detail in the complementary pack, **Handling Pressure**, available from Coachwise 1st4sport (0113-201 5555).

The two elements coaches should try to control in the environment are to reduce uncertainty and decrease importance.

However, some **uncertainty** is inherent in sport. Generally it is the uncertainty about the outcome of the competition that makes sport challenging and fun. You cannot, and should not, remove **all** this uncertainty but it is the unnecessary uncertainty which may adversely affect particular athletes that needs to be eliminated. In the following panel, you will see some examples of uncertainty in a performer's environment and suggested actions to reduce that uncertainty.

Source of uncertainty	Action to reduce uncertainty
Waiting to announce team selection until the last possible moment.	Let players know as soon as possible who will be playing.
Telling performers one thing and then doing another.	Be consistent as a coach in what you say and do.
Negative comments from the bench or crowd.	Take any action within your control to avoid threatening an athlete's self-worth.

Decreasing importance. The other cause of anxiety is the importance the performer assigns to the outcome of the competition, race or match. The outcomes may be intrinsic (ie increased self-worth, mastery experiences) or extrinsic (eg money, trophies). An important part of environmental control in this situation may involve trying to change the reactions of those people who are important to the performer in terms of the social support they provide (eg some kind of parent education meeting/programme may be useful in this situation). Although many of these factors are beyond your control and hence this approach to stress management is more limited, anything positive you or significant others can achieve will be well worth the effort. Some examples are provided in the following panel:

Source of importance	Action to reduce importance
Parents offering their children financial or other rewards.	Ask parents to discontinue this practice.
Initiate a scheme for recognising good play, causing performers to go too far.	Keep recognition in perspective, comment on performance relative to the performer's own standards.
Awards given for best player, most improved player, best attacker.	Discourage this type of reward.

Step 3: Teach anxiety management techniques

Equip performers with techniques to enable them to reduce the negative effects of both somatic and cognitive anxiety through techniques such as relaxation methods, centring and thought control[1]. A brief introduction to each is provided:

- There are many different **relaxation techniques** – some help to still the mind, which in turn relaxes the body; others reduce the excessive muscular tension which in turn calms the mind. An example of progressive muscular relaxation is provided in Programme Three (page 88) – if you are unfamiliar with this technique, try it now.

- **Centring** is really a breathing technique combined with a refocusing strategy. On inhalation, you change your centre of consciousness from your head to your centre of gravity – a point just below your navel. This lowering of your centre of consciousness helps you feel much more stable and balanced and so prompts you to relax. On exhalation, refocus your attention on the important cues that will help you to achieve the next task.

---

1   More comprehensive help on these techniques can be found in the complementary pack, **Handling Pressure**, available from Coachwise 1st4sport (0113-201 5555).

Centring

1 With your feet shoulder width apart, stand with your knees slightly bent.

2 Relax your neck, arms and shoulder muscles.

3 Direct your thoughts inward to check and adjust your muscle tension and breathing. This is best done if you focus on your abdominal muscles and how they tighten and relax as you breathe. Feel the heaviness that occurs in your muscles.

4 Take a deep, slow breath using the diaphragm (ie a point just behind your navel) with minimal movement of the chest.

5 As you continue to focus consciously on your breathing and the heaviness of your muscles, clear your mind of all irrelevant thoughts and cues.

6 Focus your thoughts on an upcoming competitive situation and what you need to do to perform effectively.

• **Thought control** is a simple technique to stop the negative thoughts and turn them into positive ones. This can be combined with positive thoughts which focus on the relevant concentration cue. For example:

Negative	*Positive*
I can't play in the wind.	*Nobody likes the wind but I know how to cope with it.*
I hope I don't choke.	*Stay cool and just watch the ball.*

Further help on thought control techniques can be found in the complementary pack **Building Self-confidence.**

Further help on these techniques is provided in Programme Three and in the complementary pack, **Handling Pressure.** It is essential that coaches talk to their performers to establish their perceptions of high arousal and the effects of anxiety on performance to establish which strategies may best be adopted to reduce the likelihood of anxiety interfering with concentration.

2.4　Controlling the Controllable

To maintain focus on the fundamental cues essential to optimal performance, performers need to concentrate on the present, the here and now, rather than allowing their concentration to drift back (eg If only I had...) or go into the future (eg What if I win...). One way to help this is to encourage the adoption of what is called a process orientation – one that focuses on the process of performing and on the aspects of performance you can control. Examples of a process orientation include focusing on the lift of the elbow in freestyle swimming, the rhythm in long distance running, the flight of the ball in tennis. Typically coaches and performers adopt an outcome orientation – focusing on the outcome (winning, losing, gaining selection) and its significance. This is not surprising for competitive sport generally has an inherent win/lose outcome – however, you cannot control the outcome.

An outcome orientation in training can be very motivating at times – for example in sports such as long-distance running, swimming or cycling which require a great deal of commitment and sacrifice, performers may motivate themselves by thinking about outcomes: 'If I win the race, I'll get a lot of media attraction'. 'By making these sacrifices, I can get the recognition and financial rewards I want'. However in competition, an outcome focus can become very negative. Thinking about the importance of winning the race or the failure that losing the race will bring, focuses attention on the things you cannot control and typically induces more anxiety, as well as shifting the focus away from the important cues.

Debbie Flintoft King, the Olympic Gold medallist for the 400m hurdles said:

> *I'm only in control of my lane so that's where I focus.*

Coaches should therefore help their performers to adopt a process orientation by setting process goals in training and competition which maintain focus on the present and are inherently more controllable than outcome goals. Performers cannot control the outcome, for this is dependent not only on how well they perform but how well the opposition performs – you can achieve a personal best and lose; you can perform badly and still win. Performers should be encouraged to focus on controlling the things they can control rather than worrying about the things they cannot – this shifts attention onto negative and probably irrelevant thoughts. In addition, if process goals are appropriately set and achieved, it is likely the outcome goals will take care of themselves.

Ain't no use worryin' bout things beyond your control, cause if they're beyond your control, ain't no use worryin'...

Ain't no use worryin' bout things within your control, cause if you got them under control, ain't no use worryin'...

A positive approach – one of self-confidence and a feeling of being in control – is more likely to facilitate concentration on the crucial factors that influence the quality of the performance. One characteristic of many people who have achieved a high level of personal success, is their ability to sort out those things they can control and to work at them, rather than concerning themselves with things which are out of their control. It is important for you as coach to identify what you can and cannot control and also to help your performers identify the controllable and uncontrollable aspects of performance. These factors within your control are the processes that will underpin good concentration. Try the next activity.

ACTIVITY 11

1   Compile a list of factors that performers in your sport can and cannot fully control:

Can Control	Cannot Control

2 Now identify the factors that you as coach can and cannot control. Remember to include factors such as other lifestyle commitments as well as time and facilities:

Can Control	Cannot Control

Now turn over.

1 *Compare your list with the following – it is not a definitive list but will give you plenty of ideas. You may also have included some more sport-specific things (eg time outs, substitution, deflections, lucky bounces):*

Can Control	Cannot Control
Concentration	Outcome of the competition
Diet – what you eat and drink	Weather
Effort and determination	Condition of the venue
Equipment	Behaviour of the opposition
Travel arrangements	Decisions of the officials
Dedication, commitment	Press/media
Discipline	Facilities
Technique	Equipment breakage/failure
Decisions	The performer's luck
Reactions to difficult situations	Illness
Time management	Spectators
Routines (eg warm-up and starting procedures)	
Fitness (injury prevention and strength/flexibility)	
PR/sponsorship campaign	
Getting time away from sport	
Attitude to mistakes (own and others)	
Communication and who you listen to	
Training programme	
Thoughts and emotions – Positive and negative	

2 *Many are inevitably the same but you may have also considered some of the following and probably more. Again there may be a number of sport-specific issues – in some sports coaches can intervene at certain times during the competition (eg at time outs in basketball and volleyball, at half time in rugby and football, between events in athletics and gymnastics):*

Can Control	Cannot Control
Organisation of the training/coaching session	The performer's motivation, effort and commitment
Punctuality	Behaviour of competitors
Value and enjoyment of the session (fun, variety)	Behaviour and decisions of officials/ other coaches
Being positive and constructive	The performance
your own emotions	The way you give feedback
The way you react to the opposition	The outcome – winning, the way you give feedback
The time you give to each performer	
The way you listen to performers	
Honesty with performers	
Your open-mindedness	
The role-model you set	
Being up to date and progressive	
Other coaches and officials	

Remember, a professional approach entails the identification and control of as many of the controllable variables in your preparation and performances as possible. It suggests you should try to cover every angle in terms of your preparation, and that each angle should be covered to the best of your ability. In other words, you should score ten out of ten on **all** the controllable factors and not worry about those you cannot control, because these will induce anxiety and distract you (and your performers) from the task. By learning to **control the controllable,** you and your performers will begin to gain and maintain an appropriate focus more consistently. In Programme Four (page 92), you will have a chance to help your performers differentiate between the controllable and uncontrollable, learn to set process goals and maintain a process orientation, and cope with distractions – even in tough situations.

Process goals should be set for training and practice sessions as well as competitions, for most good performers spend more time practising than competing. This will help focus attention on the goals during the session. Crib cards (written reminders on postcards or post-its) may be used – these should carry no more than three or four key words or phrases that remind the performer where to focus his or her thoughts.

> *Stay in the here and now.*

2.5 Developing Routines

Routines can help focus or refocus attention. Elite performers seem to adopt well-learnt and consistent routines they execute each and every time they prepare for and perform during competitions – imagine the sprinter going down onto the blocks, the basketball player on the free throw line or the golfer on the tee. They seem to do the same things, in the same order and with the same timing. If you look more closely, you may notice that many teams apparently go through the same ritual prior to every match, as do track and field athletes, gymnasts and cyclists. If you want to produce consistent, high quality performances every time you compete, you must have a consistent base from which to perform. Elite performers, unlike novices, seem to develop these rituals or habits which might include technical, physical and psychological routines. They may provide some security through familiarity, they may ensure you control all the variables you can, and also ensure a sound focus on the right things at the right time. Not only will this benefit performance, it will also help to negate the distractions and potential negative thoughts that may otherwise invade the mind.

Pre-competition routines

Routines break preparation down into a sequence of events (sometimes known as performance segmenting) which help maintain this psychological control which boosts confidence and concentration, and controls emotions and thought processes. Most sports performers develop some form of routine for competition days. This may include specific activities on the night before competition, the morning of the competition, during warm-ups, the competition itself or post-competition (these types of routines will be looked at specifically in Programme Five, page 97).

The most important element of the immediate pre-competition warm-up routines is to help the performer attain his or her *ideal performance state (IPS)*. This refers to the state of activation or readiness of the mind and body necessary to produce optimal performance. This state will vary from sport to sport as well as from one performer to another[1]. Most coaches subscribe to the need to prepare the body for action – gain the appropriate physical IPS prior to competition – but less consideration is often afforded the specific tactical, technical or psychological demands of the forthcoming event. How many times have you seen performers or teams physically ready but mentally not switched on? How often are opportunities lost or goals conceded early on? It appears the performers were not in their IPS – certainly in terms of their psychological readiness to read situations, make decisions and effect techniques competently.

A key element of a pre-competition warm-up routine therefore will integrate the desired physical, psychological, technical and tactical component into a comprehensive programme that suits the individual performer. Study the following examples of an integrated pre-competition routine for a table tennis player and a pursuit cyclist.

Time Before Start	Activity
	Review match tactics Review process goals Focus on best performance imagery
	Knock-up and stretching
	Go to the toilet
8 Mins	Relax Shadow play
2 Mins	Remember cue words: tactical – early ball emotional – be tough psychological – next point

Figure 4: Example of an integrated warm-up routine for a table tennis player

1   For further information, refer to the complementary pack, **Handling Pressure**, available from Coachwise 1st4sport (0113-201 5555).

Time	Activity
12.00 noon	Sleep
3.00 pm	Dress, eat and travel to the track
4.00 pm	Go to the changing room
4.10 pm	Have a massage
4.30 pm	Listen to relaxation tape
5.00 pm	Remember imagery
5.15 pm	Warm-up on king cycle
6.00 pm	Change – rubber suit
6.10 pm	Go to middle of the track
6.30 pm	Acclimatise to the environment
6.40 pm	Go on rollers – listen to arousal tape
6.55 pm	Rub down – put suit on
7.00 pm	To the line – centring – cue words.

Figure 5: Pre-race routine for a pursuit cyclist

Note that the routines in the examples are very different in many ways. Many of the components may be determined by the nature of the sport, the nature of the positional role a player has in the team or the needs of the individual. This suggests that routines will usually differ between sports, may differ for different positions within a team and almost certainly for different individuals.

It is important to construct and then practise a pre-competition focusing routine to meet the specific needs of both the situation and the performer. The next activity will help you start to think about the important components.

ACTIVITY 12

Outline the important components of a pre-competition routine for a typical performer in your sport. You may wish to start this routine the night before the event or deal more specifically with the immediate pre-competition time:

Time Before Start	Activity

This activity will have helped you to think through all the elements that need to be considered. However, it is only a blueprint and needs to be developed and adapted to meet the specific and unique needs of each performer. If you are coaching teams, you will need to make further adjustments to cater for the needs of each individual player as well as the overall preparation of the team. This may demand some negotiation and clear recognition of individual needs as well as team needs. Programme Five on page 97 will help you develop and implement individual pre-competition routines.

You should try to ensure this routine is catered for whenever your performer is competing at home or away (eg staying in a hotel, travelling to a new venue). This may mean checking meal menus, identifying travel options and checking the venue (eg to identify quiet places where your performer can relax before the event). Knowing this has been done enables your performer to focus on his/her preparation and arrive at the event as well prepared as possible.

Some coaches and performers believe that a more detailed preparation phase over a longer time-frame is important in helping to focus performers on the competition and ensure their IPS can be attained in the immediate pre-competition phase. Study the example in the next panels. Note that the coach and sailor have divided or segmented the preparation phase into six segments. The aim is to control the controllables, minimise anxiety and help to focus attention on the important cues at every stage.

Segment 1: Night before the competition

Things to do:
1 Prepare equipment – check boat, sails and spares.
2 Have a relaxation period – listen to music, read, watch TV or socialise.
3 Review tactics – start strategies, race tactics, venue related issues.
4 Check for sailing instruction amendments (if appropriate).
5 Do progressive muscle relaxation (use prepared tape) and mental rehearsal of start strategies.
6 Follow go-to-sleep strategy.

Segment 2: From waking up until moving to the venue

Things to do:
1 Follow wake up routine.
2 Stretch and mentally rehearse.
3 Ring for weather forecast.
4 Eat breakfast.
5 Prepare food and drink for the day (and between races).
6 Pack gear.
7 Leave for the venue.

Segment 3: From arrival at venue until setting sail

Things to do:
1 Arrive at the venue at predetermined time (ie not too long beforehand).
2 Perform a technical check – equipment, course, official meteorology, notice board.
3 Perform a tactical check – race details, points situation, last review of tactics with coach or crew (as desired).
4 Relax and remember best performance imagery.
5 Warm-up, stretch and use key words.
6 Set sail.

Segment 4: Pre-race routine

Things to do:
1 Check the relevance of the forecast and current.

2 Adjust clothing.

3 Execute pre-start routine:
- Check for start line bias.
- Establish transit (if appropriate).
- Check up the first beat.
- Check 'time on distance' at start line.

Segment 5: Between races

Things to do:
1 Modify rig settings.

2 Modify techniques.

3 Modify course – which side paid?

4 Talk to other people – such as coach, sailors (to check 1, 2, and 3).

5 Eat and drink.

Segment 6: Post-performance

Things to do:
1 Highlight good aspects of performance and record in diary.

2 Highlight poor aspects of performance and record in diary.

3 Eat and drink (as soon as possible after the finish of the last race).

4 Check equipment.

5 Check for protests.

6 Plan evening (eg meal/social activities).

This type of detailed performance segmenting can be developed with your performer by following these steps:

1   Determine the **start time and a finish point** for the plan – remember you can plan for some eventualities during the performance and you can certainly plan for most eventualities after the competition. Therefore most plans should have the before, during and after elements outlined.

2   List the parts or **segments** in your plan. The number of segments will depend on just how detailed you want the plan to be and how long a period is to be covered by the plan.

3   **Record the segments** on paper and on an audiotape. Try to ensure this can readily be adapted – you may find you want to add or amend segments or items.

4   **Learn your plan.** Pin it up somewhere prominent – on the fridge, mirror, wall. Practise it in training and minor competitions.

5   **Fine tune your plan** – be prepared to make changes as it develops. As it becomes more automatic, you will find you can afford to simplify it – for example by replacing a phrase in the plan with a single cue word. These cue words can become crib cards and prove a much more efficient way of creating the right image (for imagery), feelings or perhaps arousal level.

6   **Take your plan to competitions** – you never know when you might need to refer to it.

Refocusing routines

As important as focusing before the start of competition is the ability to refocus during an event – routines can also be used effectively within the competition. Performers may have specific routines before individual techniques (eg the kicker in rugby may take a set number of steps backward, focus on the posts, take a deep breath, imagine the ball passing through the posts, use a trigger word or concentration cue to relax before taking the kick). Similarly during a competition or training session if focus is lost, a breathe-focus-act routine can help to refocus (see panel over page). There will be numerous occasions when performers will need to block out distractions and concentrate on a specific skill or aspect of the performance.

The **Breathe-Focus-Act** refocusing routine can be learnt, practised and refined in training:

1 **Breathe** – focus on the movement of the chest, take in a long slow breath, hold for a silent count of three, relax and breathe out slowly. Repeat.

   This takes away the focus from the distraction (internal or external) onto the movement of the chest and restores a feeling of control to the performer.

2 **Focus** – use a concentration or performance cue word/phrase/picture to take the performer back into the performance and the here and now.

3 **Act** – focus shift onto doing rather than thinking.

Once learnt, it can be used in low level competitions and finally at critical moments in important competitions.

This type of routine can be adjusted to suit the sport situation and the performer. For example in tennis, an alternative or supplementary first physical action might be to adjust the strings on the racket, the second focus might be a physical action such as bouncing the ball three times and the third execution stage might involve instructional words such as *smooth but powerful*. It is important to establish the content and format of a refocusing routine that is appropriate for your performer(s) in your sport. You will have a chance to do this in Programme Five (page 97). Try the next activity.

ACTIVITY 13

Identify potential situations in competition in your sport when a performance routine might be used to focus or refocus concentration (consider specific situations such as re-start situations as well as predictable events such as after a mistake):

-

-

-

-

-

-

Now turn over.

Routines can be used effectively in an intermittent type of sport when there are natural breaks in the action which may:

- *be programmed, such as at half time, end of a game, set or round*

- *be dictated by the coach, such as timeouts, substitutions*

- *be determined by officials, such as when play is briefly suspended (ball out of play, fouls, an injury, penalty)*

- *occur naturally – between points (racket games), deliveries (cricket, baseball), attempts (field events in athletics, target sports, golf), rounds (diving) or events (gymnastics).*

Other key times when they could be used might be:

- *after a mistake (own or others)*

- *whenever distracted*

- *after an official's unfavourable decision*

- *after a goal (conceded or scored)*

- *when tired, anxious, frustrated.*

Having identified with your performers appropriate opportunities in your sport to focus and refocus, it is important to construct a personalised routine to meet the specific needs of both the situation and the performer. You will have a chance to do this with your performer in Programme Five (page 97). This then needs to be developed to ensure ultimately the performer can call upon quick and effective refocusing routines even in the heat of competition.

For dealing with more emotive situations (eg after being shown a yellow card in soccer or falling from the beam in gymnastics), there may be a need to start the routine with some form of thought-stopping technique. This is simply using a word such as *stop* or *change* to halt the negative thought and help move into the predetermined routine. Similarly a visual rather than verbal thought stopping trigger can be used. Some examples are provided in the panel on the opposite page.

Routines can be used very effectively to deal with mistakes. Typically many performers experience difficulty in eliminating them from their minds – they prey on their minds. An interesting technique that has been used quite successfully has been termed *error parking*[1]. The performer is encouraged to create an image which successfully disposes of the error. They quote an international rower who turned errors into stones which could be tossed over into the water to sink out of sight; a professional golfer who imagined filing errors into a cabinet and shutting the drawer. These routines which demand some imagery skills (see Section 2.6) need to be rehearsed so they develop an automatic link between error and image, and then image and refocus onto relevant cues.

In addition to these short-term refocusing techniques, before the competition you can also identify the important task-relevant performance cues to use if you become distracted or need to develop an alternative strategy.

Post-competition routines can be effective in some sports (eg target sports) to ensure the greatest possible benefit can be gained from the performance – by continually eliminating the poor and reproducing the good, more consistent performance should ensue. This analysis may involve an evaluation of technical, tactical and physical elements of performance, but within the mental/psychological assessment, the identification of where errors have occurred and the role that concentration mismatch has played during the competition will be critical. A greater awareness of strengths and weaknesses within your concentration will be an important part of your overall performance analysis strategy.

It is important to recognise the need for flexibility within the routine, in case uncontrollable elements compromise the timing of its execution. This is important for pre-competition routines which may need to be adapted due to unforeseen late arrival at the venue (eg the bus breaks down) or rescheduling of the start time (eg due to weather). The routine should build in various means of coping with unexpected eventualities (the what-ifs). Routines used within the competition may also need to be flexible – particularly in the more open activities and sports where the timing cannot always be controlled by the performer (eg at an injury delay in field games).

---

1   Bull, S., Albinson, J. and Shambrook, C. (1996) **The Mental Game Plan.**

ACTIVITY 14

Study the following examples and then add your own what-ifs and suggest appropriate contingencies:

What-ifs	Contingency
Delayed start time	*Have a book or radio with you (prevents boredom and provides an effective relaxation technique – a positive distraction)*
Delayed arrival at venue	*Use imagery drills as a mental warm-up and a short version of the physical warm-up.*

Programme Five, page 97 will provide guidance on how to develop, practise and implement routines with your performers and how to identify and practise contingencies so the performer is able to focus and refocus effectively irrespective of the situation.

2.6   Using Imagery

Imagery involves creating a clear mental picture – of the venue, the performance, the conditions, the people. This skill underpins many mental training techniques and strategies and can be a vital part of the performer's mental kit bag. Often imagery relies most strongly on the visual image but it is generally accepted that the more senses evoked (sound, smell, touch, feel, taste), the more powerful the imagery. Some examples of each sensory input are provided in the following panel.

Sense	Example
Sight	Venue, conditions, equipment, opposition, movements, officials, spectators
Hearing	Sound of own breathing, opponent's calls, officials, spectators, equipment, coach
Touch/feeling	Feel of equipment, body sensations (muscle, joint, balance) associated with movement, warmth/rain/wind
Smell	Wet grass, leather ball, sea breeze, embrocation
Taste	Own sweat, gum shield, chlorinated water

Stop to think of the pertinent stimuli in your sport in the first exercise in the following activity. If you are unfamiliar with the skill of imagery, work through Exercises 2–4.

ACTIVITY 15

1   Identify a task or skill from your own sport and describe a range of sensations associated with it. It might help to think of a specific occasion when you carried out this task or skill successfully:

Sight:

Hearing:

Touch:

Smell:

Taste:

2   Read the following instructions carefully so you are familiar with them:

Preparation: Make yourself comfortable in a chair.

Exercise: Take in a long slow breath, hold for a silent count of three, relax and breathe out slowly. Repeat twice and close your eyes. Think of a pleasant sporting occasion where you performed well. Run the image through your mind at normal speed until you reach the end or until your concentration wavers. Count from one to three and open your eyes.

Now try the exercise.

3 After the exercise, answer the following questions:

How vividly were you able to experience the event?

Very ☐   Somewhat ☐   Not very well ☐   Not at all ☐

Which senses were you able to evoke?

Sight ☐   Sound ☐   Feel/touch ☐   Smell ☐

Did you experience the events as though you were there – seeing, hearing and feeling everything through your own senses as it happened (this is referred to as internal imagery)?   Yes / No

Did you experience the events as if you were watching a film or video, like a recording of yourself carrying out the action (this is referred to as external imagery)?   Yes / No

Did you switch between the two types?   Yes / No

4 You may wish to repeat the whole exercise again.

NB Like any other skill, plenty of practice is needed to develop and hone the skill of imagery – short bursts (five to ten minute sessions) seem to be most effective.

Imagery can be used for a variety of purposes – for example to:

- accelerate the learning or honing of skills
- build or restore confidence
- rehearse the correct technique or strategy
- practise identifying the relevant attentional cues to facilitate decision-making
- provide feedback to reinforce the good and identify and rectify errors
- focus attention on task-relevant cues and so improve concentration.

The main advantage of imagery is that it allows performers to practise in any location at any time. As a tool to improve concentration and to facilitate refocusing, it is very powerful and should form an integral part of many of the other skills already considered (eg routines, identifying and using concentration cues, controlling anxiety). For example, to:

- practise attending to your concentration cues in specific situations and enjoying the successful performance that ensues – this can be particularly beneficial if the performer learns to visualise successful performance in situations they find most distracting and difficult to handle

- rehearse the use of refocusing routines – for example after a mistake to help turn failure into success.

Remember that imagery, like any other skill, needs to be maintained through regular practise several times a week.

2.7   Distraction Training

Self-evaluation can be one of the greatest internal distractions – one or two errors are quickly generalised into an overall self-judgement of poor performance with the consequential loss of attention on the important cues. Gallwey's (1975) *Inner Game* approach suggested that this type of judgemental thinking leads to impaired performance because as he explains, *the brain starts to override your body and this results in trying too hard, tightening of muscles and tentative performance – there is a loss of rhythm, timing and smoothness.* He advocates the need to develop the skill of relaxed concentration (sometimes termed passive concentration) and claims the secret of winning in sport lies in not trying too hard. This is very much in line with a process orientation rather than an outcome orientation. He uses drills which focus attention away from judgemental issues onto very focused concentration cues (such as watching the seam of the tennis ball or calling *bounce* as it hits the ground, focusing on the sensation in the shoulder in the back swing in golf or rating the smoothness of the action on a five point scale). All distract the mind from self-instruction, trying too hard or judgemental behaviour.

By simulating situations in which external distractions interfere with concentration, you can help performers practise using strategies to help them stay focused. This type of work is sometimes referred to as distraction simulation training and can be used effectively with a little imagination to replicate the classic situations when distractions occur (or even specific distractions at particular venues). A number of distraction examples are given in the following table, together with examples of how simulated training might be conducted.

Distraction	Simulation
Spectators – a large crowd, a noisy crowd, a hostile crowd. This can be distracting and may be sufficiently loud to interfere.	This can be simulated at training sessions using an audiotape of crowd noise on a public address system.
Another source of noise – such as a nearby railway track, overhead flight path, industrial estate, road works.	Similarly, an audiotape can be used in practice situations or practice can be carried out at a venue where the noise occurs.
Opponents – perhaps verbal or physical abuse, professional fouls or cheating.	This can be simulated in training by directing certain players to react in particular ways to other unsuspecting players who struggle with maintaining focus against unsporting behaviour by other players.
Officials – particularly in relation to unfavourable decisions.	Bad calls can be introduced into practise games at crucial times and players helped to cope and retain focus.
Uncontrollable or bad luck situations – such as equipment failure (archery), bad bounces and net cords (tennis), unfavourable deflections (soccer, hockey) losing a key player through injury or fouls.	Some of these can be manufactured to occur, others you will need to capitalise on as and when they occur.
Overload – too much information, too little time to react, too many choices.	This can be done through devising practices that put increasing demands on performers (eg two or more people feeding balls in quick succession, feeding awkward balls, giving too many instructions at a timeout) – be careful to ensure the practice is still safe.

2.8   Summary and Further Help

In this chapter you have been introduced to the concept of concentration in sport. Individual concentration differences, the varying concentration requirements of different sports and common attentional/concentration problems were also outlined. You have also considered six mental skills selected to improve concentration: identifying concentration cues, arousal control, process orientation, routines, imagery and performance planning. Each skill was outlined to highlight its potential use to improve concentration. In the next chapter, you will be encouraged to analyse the strengths and weaknesses of your performers so you can identify the most appropriate mental skills for each of them.

Further help on mental skills work, and in particular on the mental skills discussed, can be found in:

Bull S., Albinson J. and Shambrook C. (1996) **The Mental Game Plan: Getting Psyched for Sport.** Cheltenham: Sports Dynamics. ISBN 0-9519543-2-6

Gallwey, W.T. (1997) **The Inner Game of Tennis.** London: Redwood Burn Limited. ISBN 0-224-01178-2

Morris, T. (1997) **Psychological Skills Training in Sport: An Overview.** (2nd edition) Leeds: Coachwise Solutions/The National Coaching Foundation. ISBN 0-947850-783

Sellars, C . (2004) **Mental Skills: An Introduction for Sports Coaches.** Leeds: Coachwise Solutions/The National Coaching Foundation. ISBN 0-947850-34-1

Chapter Three: Profiling your Performer

3.0 What's in It for You?

Having considered the essential mental qualities for successful sports performance and some of the techniques that might be used to develop these qualities, you now need to identify the specific needs of your performers. What are their strengths and weaknesses? How good at concentration are they? How might the needs of one performer differ from another?

In this chapter you will use the technique of performance profiling[1] to examine the factors that influence success in your sport and to assess your performer's strengths and weaknesses against this profile. (If you are familiar with the technique, you may wish to skim this section.) Although the technique is used to profile every aspect of performance (physical, technical, tactical and mental), the emphasis will be placed on the mental factors (particularly the role of concentration) and an evaluation of the extent to which your performers currently use mental skills. By the end of this chapter, you should be able to:

- profile the qualities needed to improve competitive performance in one of your athletes
- identify with your performer the mental skills needed to develop these essential qualities
- assess your performer's current use of selected mental skills and agree priorities
- use performance profiling to monitor the development of mental skills (especially those concerned with improved concentration)
- select which mental skills training programmes will be most suitable for your performer
- determine when you should embark on any form of mental skills work.

---

1 This is a technique developed by Richard Butler. For further guidance on this technique, you are recommended to look at the **sports coach UK** pack and workshop **Performance Profiling**, available from Coachwise 1st4sport (0113-201 5555).

3.1 How to Profile

Most coaches assess their performers' strengths and weaknesses but often in an *ad hoc* way and sometimes without keeping a record of these assessments. One more systematic method gaining popularity with coaches is that of performance profiling. This technique enables both the coach and performer to record their respective assessments of the performer's ability on each key aspect of performance.

ACTIVITY 16

1 In relation to one of your performers (Performer A), make a list of the ten factors that contribute most significantly to his/her performance level (it will help if you think of specific performances and consider technical/tactical, physical and mental factors). List these in the left-hand column (leave all the other columns blank):

Performer A	Rank	Performer B	Rank

2   Record what you notice about the qualities in your list:

- What is the balance in terms of physical, technical/tactical and mental factors?

- Which ones change over time?

- How many are controllable by you or your performer?

3   Focus on the mental qualities you listed and consider the following:

- How important is mental toughness – the four Cs in your list (confidence, concentration, control and commitment)?

- Did you mention concentration directly or indirectly? Do you think this should be on your list?

- Note any other observations:

4   If necessary, go back and amend the qualities listed in Question 1.

Now turn over.

You have now started the profiling process.

1   *You might like to compare your factors with the qualities you generated in Activity 1 in the first chapter (page 2).*

2   *You may wish to reflect on the relative importance given to mental factors in relation to physical and technical/tactical ones. How different might the factors be in relation to another performer?*

If your list consisted of predominantly controllable factors (those that can be influenced by you or your performer), then you will be able to adapt your coaching sessions to bring about suitable changes. If your list was full of uncontrollable factors (eg the weather, opponents), you and your performer may become demoralised and lose confidence with your inability to bring about change (when required).

If your list has more than five uncontrollable factors, go back and check if you omitted any controllable factors that had a significant influence.

3   *Concentration may well have appeared on your list, for most performers suffer fluctuations in concentration. If it did, you can be sure that this person's performance will benefit from improved concentration. However, even if concentration did not appear directly, it will inevitably have influenced some of the factors you listed. Go back to your list in Question 1 and underline the factors influenced by concentration.*

Performance profiling will help you and your performer identify the most important influences on performance. By doing this, you will be able to prioritise areas on which to work and therefore better inform your coaching programmes (eg your prioritisation will help determine long- and short-term objectives). A performer's profile is, however, very individual. To contrast the similarities and differences, try the next activity.

ACTIVITY 17

1   Repeat Activity 16 for another of your performers (Performer B) and record the factors in the right-hand column on page 64.

2   For each performer, now rank the relative importance of the ten factors using the column marked **rank** (ie if power is deemed the most important, rank it as 1, if concentration is the next most important, rank it as 2, and so on). NB Even if some of the qualities are the same, the ranking may be different.

3   Contrast your two lists and summarise the similarities and differences:

4   Note the relative importance of concentration:

You probably found that even if your lists contained many similar factors, they may have been ranked quite differently. This is perfectly natural but does highlight the importance of treating each performer as an individual. If the key factors that influence the two performers are ranked differently, this may need to be reflected in the training programme and the coaching methods used. It may be only after such an exercise that these differences are apparent (to you and your performers).

Having looked more closely at the factors or qualities that influence success for each of your performers and perhaps focused more clearly on mental qualities, you should discuss these with your performers – their thoughts on the most significant ten qualities and their relative importance to success. You will have a chance to do this in Programme One, page 74.

3.2 Why Profile?

Performance profiling is an excellent technique to help coaches and performers to:

- identify the important components of performance
- clarify and agree training and competition priorities
- set goals
- monitor the success of their coaching.

To be effective, ensure you observe the following guidelines.

Guidelines for using performance profiling

- Use performance profiling to identify and record your own and your performer's targets for mental skills training.
- Agree with your performer his/her current level of performance at key mental skills.
- Use the performance profiling process to form the basis of long- and medium-term goal-setting.
- Performance profiling can be used as part of your ongoing monitoring of mental skills (do not overuse).

3.3 When to Profile

Be careful you do not misuse performance profiling by using it too often. An example of the frequency of profiling is shown in Figure 6 (although this will vary according to your needs).

Month	J	F	M	A	M	J	J	A	S	O	N	D
Phase	Competitive season				Rest	Pre-season			Early competitive season			
Profile		✔				1st			✔			✔

Figure 6: Example of profiling frequency (rugby union)

ACTIVITY 18

Now complete a similar chart for your sport. Mark on the chart the phases of your competitive year. Indicate when in the year you will profile your performer (this will need to be flexible as circumstances may change):

Month	J	F	M	A	M	J	J	A	S	O	N	D
Phase												
Profile												

NB You may wish to refer back to Activity 3 on page 11 where you identified when mental skills training would be introduced into your training programme.

Programme One (page 74) should be completed at the point identified in Activity 14 as most appropriate for initial profiling.

3.4 Your Performer

Before embarking on the programmes in Part Two, you should reflect on the concentration ability of your performers and the mental skills they may currently employ (consciously or largely unconsciously). The next activity may be helpful.

ACTIVITY 19

Answer the following questions about your performer (if you intend to work with more than one performer, you will either need to use a different coloured pen or photocopy this activity):

1   I would rate my performer's general ability to
    concentrate in training situations as: high/good/unstable/poor/low.

    I would rate my performer's general ability to
    concentrate in competitions as: high/good/unstable/poor/low.

2   You may wish to ask your performers to rate their ability to concentrate in a particular situation (eg a particular training session or element; a competition) – either by placing a mark on a scale such as:

    Good concentration ←————————————————→ Poor concentration

    or by using faces such as:

3   You might rate your performer's ability to use different mental skills by completing the following:

    My performer can use:

    - **concentration cues**   very well/quite well/somewhat/a little/not at all
    - **relaxation training**   very well/quite well/somewhat/a little/not at all
    - **process goals**   very well/quite well/somewhat/a little/not at all
    - **routines**   very well/quite well/somewhat/a little/not at all
    - **imagery**   very well/quite well/somewhat/a little/not at all.

4   My performer uses:

    - **concentration cues**   always/frequently/sometimes/rarely/never
    - **relaxation training**   always/frequently/sometimes/rarely/never
    - **process goals**   always/frequently/sometimes/rarely/never
    - **routines**   always/frequently/sometimes/rarely/never
    - **imagery**   always/frequently/sometimes/rarely/never.

3.5 Summary and Further Help

In this chapter you have been introduced to performance profiling as a technique to help you identify with your performers their relative strengths and weaknesses and so help you to prioritise training needs and set appropriate goals. You have used this technique to identify significant performance qualities and identify one quality which, when improved, will positively influence concentration. The means by which this quality can be improved is the subject of the remainder of this pack. You may already have decided that certain mental skills seem more appropriate for your needs than others.

If you wish to know more about the technique of profiling, you are strongly encouraged to read one or more of the following:

Butler, R. (1996) **Performance Profiling.** Leeds: Coachwise Solutions/The National Coaching Foundation. ISBN 0-947850-36-8 (Tape and booklet).

Sellars, C. (2004) **Mental Skills: An Introduction for Sports Coaches.** Leeds: Coachwise Solutions/The National Coaching Foundation. ISBN 0-947850-34-1

Programmes to Improve Concentration

Introduction

Having worked through Part One, you should now have an understanding of what is meant by good concentration, the sorts of problems that can arise and some of the strategies that might be employed with your performers to improve their ability to gain and maintain the appropriate focus. You may already have some insights about which strategies you feel might be most beneficial to your performer. In Part Two, you will find eight programmes to use with your performer to improve concentration. You are recommended to start with the first one which involves a profiling exercise as this may well influence your programme selection subsequently.

The programmes progress through similar stages:

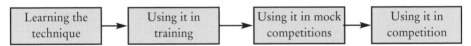

Figure 7: Stages in completing mental skills programme

Help will also be given on ways to monitor and evaluate the programme, as well as assess its relative value to performance.

Programme One: Profiling your Performer

AIM

To help coaches and performers use performance profiling to identify the qualities needed to improve concentration.

In Activity 16 (page 64), you were encouraged to draw up the ten most important factors for success for two specific performers you coach. In this programme you will develop this further, working with your performer(s) to build up a profile and identify the strategy which, with improvement, will contribute most to improved concentration.

By the end of this programme, you should be able to use profiling to:

- assess your performers' ability to concentrate – particularly in difficult situations
- assess your performers' ability to use a range of mental skills and strategies
- determine how you will help them to improve their concentration in the short-medium-term (within two to three months).

In this programme, you will need to work with your performers on one occasion outside coaching for between one and two hours.

Outside coaching session (1–2 hours)

☐ Ask your performer/s to write down the ten most important qualities they feel contribute to their success in sport. Discuss these qualities with them and share your ideas (from Activity 16, page 64). You will need to come to some consensus about the ten. Try to establish what exactly your performer means by a certain quality (it may be different from your meaning).

Quality (Generated by Performer)	Description of Quality (by Performer)
Example from tennis: *concentration in tight situations*	*Focusing on the right tactics in critical situations (eg at game points and tie-breaks)*

Keep this record of the meaning of these significant qualities – you will need to refer back to it later.

CORNWALL COLLEGE
LEARNING CENTRE

2   Using these qualities as labels, complete the outer ring of the profile in Figure 8
     (if you have less than ten labels, you can leave some blank or agree additional
     labels to add):

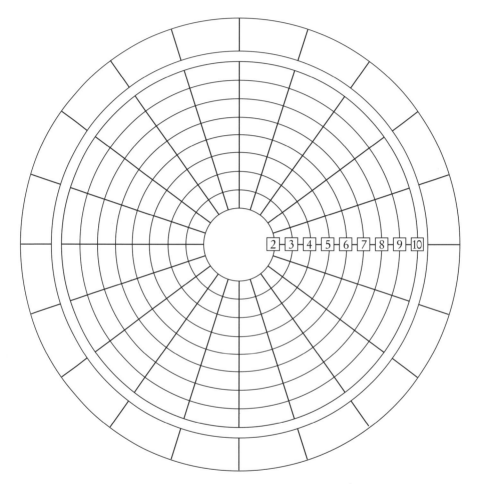

Figure 8: Profile of your performer[1]

3   Agree with your performer the ideal score (out of ten) on each of these qualities
     (ie identify the ultimate goal for this performer). Look first at Figure 9.

---

1   Profiles used for performance profiling often have more than 10 sectors/factors. However, for the purpose of
    this activity, 10 will be adequate. NB Before writing, you may wish to photocopy this profile for future use.

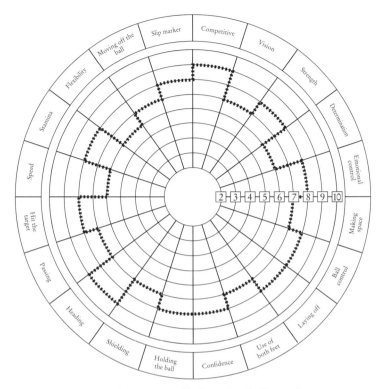

Figure 9: Profile for a football attacker

4   Mark your agreed *ideal* scores for this performer on your profile in Figure 8.

5   For each of the qualities in your profile, agree your performer's current level and mark these in a different colour on your profile (your performer should lead this part of the profiling as it is his/her perceptions of competence that will influence significantly concentration level).

6   The difference between these two sets of scores identifies the improvements needed in each of the qualities[1]. For each of your qualities, record the difference between the two scores (ideal and current) in the table over the page.

---

1   For more detail on how to use performance profiling, refer to the **sports coach UK** Performance Profiling booklet and workshop (log on to www.sportscoachUK.org/improve/workshop/search.asp).

Qualities	Ideal Score	Current Score	Difference

7   Ask the performer to consider his/her score for concentration or a similar quality such as focused, in touch or tune, in the zone. If concentration has not been listed as a key quality, you will need to consider why it has been omitted. It is unlikely to be unimportant in your sport; it is more likely that it has either been forgotten (in which case you may need to raise this) or the performer is so strong in this quality that it has been overlooked.

Try to tease out a little more about what the performer understands by good and poor concentration (remember to use the performer's word if it is different), where it should be in particular situations, when it is good, when it is poor, where it goes when it is poor.

	Good Concentration	Poor Concentration
Characteristics:		
Situations when it occurs:		
Focus of attention:		

8   Ask the performer how he/she currently deals with concentration difficulties and distractions at present. It may help to identify commonly occurring situations such as at the start, after a break, towards the end (or more sport-specific ones such as after a goal, when a foul is called against you, after a mistake). You may wish to profile concentration skills in different situations. First brainstorm on the situations in which concentration is a key factor to success. Place these on the perimeter of the following profile and then ask the performer to assess his/her ability to concentrate in each situation.

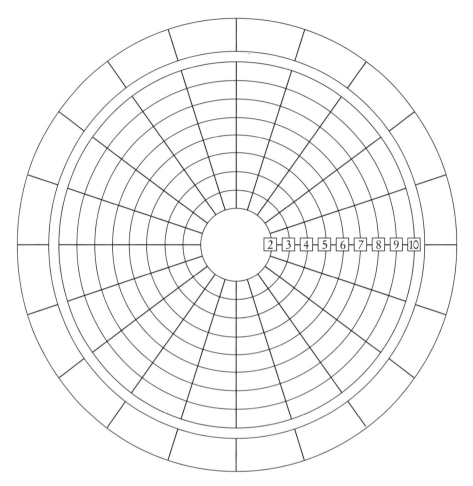

Ask the performer to identify one or more situations in which he or she would most like to see some improvement and agree how much improvement would be required to result in greater confidence in gaining and maintaining concentration in the specified situation/s (eg if currently a 6, will achieving a 7 suffice?). Check it is challenging but attainable; then complete the table on the opposite page[1].

1   You may wish to adapt this record sheet to suit your own needs.

Name:		Date:	
Situation selected:			
Current rating:		Ideal score:	
Improvement agreed:		Time-frame:	
Situation selected:			
Current rating:		Ideal score:	
Improvement agreed:		Time-frame:	
Situation selected:			
Current rating:		Ideal score:	
Improvement agreed:		Time-frame:	

As before, agree the ideal score, current score and the differential between the two. This will help you to select suitable programmes from which your performer might benefit.

Situation	Ideal Score	Current Score	Difference

9   Try to establish whether or not any use is made of mental skills such as routines, relaxation techniques, imagery and concentration cues to aid concentration in any of the identified situations:

Situation	Mental Skill Used

You may be able to combine this with Step 10 which assesses the performer's current use of each mental skill.

10 You may wish to profile your performer's current experience and use of the mental skills used in this pack to help improve concentration. If so, draw up a profile of mental skills which might enhance concentration and encourage your performer to add any additional labels.

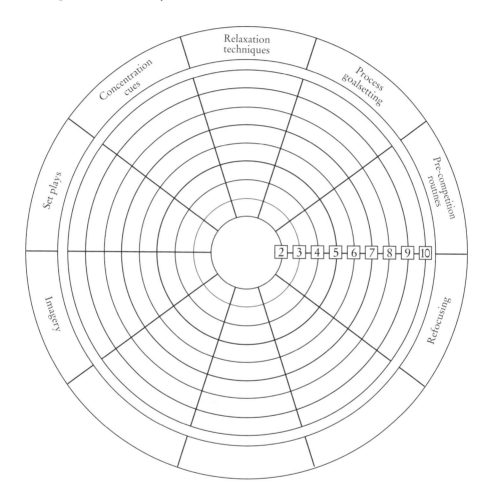

Relaxation techniques

Concentration cues

Process goalsetting

Set plays

Pre-competition routines

Imagery

Refocusing

2—3—4—5—6—7—8—9—10

Figure 10: Profile of mental qualities and skills

Programme Two: Improving Concentration by using Performance Cues

AIM

To help the performer identify where attention should be placed during performance.

You often hear coaches telling players to concentrate. This not only tells the player nothing but may also cause performance to deteriorate – the performer may try too hard or start to focus on the negative consequences of not concentrating well. Learning to concentrate is learning what to focus on in order to make a skilled response. The advice needed from the coach is not therefore to concentrate or concentrate harder (for you know concentration should be relaxed and easy); the coach should give advice about where concentration should be focused in various situations and how distractions may best be handled.

In the first programme (page 74), you and your performer began to identify the critical situations in your sport where concentration is crucial. These may be situations which are:

- characteristically difficult in most sports (eg immediately prior to the start when anxiety may be high, after an error, when the score line is critical, after an unexpected break such as for an injury)

- highly specific to your own sport (eg tie-break in tennis, penalty in soccer or hockey, final lap in a middle or long distance event)

- identified by your performer as key or problematic (eg before the parallel bar exercise, the final turn, when serving at set point up or down, after being called for a foul).

Before embarking on this programme, ensure you have read the section on concentration cues in Chapter Two (page 28). By the end of this programme, you should be able to:

- identify important concentration cues for critical elements of your sport
- devise practices and simulated training situations to reinforce the use of these cues.

In this programme, you will need to work with your performers on one occasion outside coaching for between one and two hours, then regularly in practice sessions and ultimately a competitive situation.

Phase A: Outside coaching session (1–2 hours)

Using one of the critical situations elicited by your performer in Programme One, ask your performer to imagine the situation in as much detail as possible. If your performer is skilled at using imagery, use both internal and external imagery to try to picture the situation. Use prompts to try to elicit what he/she sees, hears, feels (kinaesthetic) and thinks, both when the performance is going well and concentration is easily gained and maintained, and when concentration strays. Jot down everything shared.

What the performer:	Concentration Good	Concentration Poor
sees		
hears		
feels		
thinks		

2   Using the information gained, encourage the performer to identify cue words
     which represent the cues that describe performance when concentration is
     appropriately focused. These may be verbal, visual or physical and may be:

     •   instructional (eg at the start of a sprint race: a verbal cue such as *explode* or a
         visual cue such as a panther crouched and ready to pounce)

     •   motivational (eg during a gymnastics routine, use of the words *go for it* or a
         particular sound such as a drum roll)

     •   emotional (eg saying *relax*, or physical – taking a deep breath and bouncing
         the ball three times)

     •   psychological (eg telling yourself to *stay in the here and now* to refocus or
         watching the seams on the ball in flight).

Notice whether the performer tends to choose a particular type of cue – physical,
verbal, auditory or visual. It is beneficial to help performers identify as many of
the fundamental foci as possible. However, remember that this should be a gradual
process, so keep the cues as few and simple as possible. The cues they use must be
meaningful to the performer – his/her choice, not those of the coach.

Situation	Fundamental Focus	Cue

Phase B: Subsequent work in practice sessions and ultimately a competitive situation

1   The next step is to devise sessions in practice when the situation identified can be replicated as realistically as possible. The performer can then be encouraged to try using the trigger and perhaps rating the effectiveness of the concentration during the subsequent performance. It may be helpful to encourage performers to rate their concentration after each or a number of attempts. It is important to assess the effectiveness of the trigger but not to become too bogged down on evaluation.

2   Finally, once the strategy is working well in training, you can start to introduce it in competition – relatively unimportant ones first, then gradually starting to use it in all competitions. Again keep monitoring the performer's ability to gain and maintain the relevant focus and use whatever reminders have proven useful. Once the performer has mastered one situation, you may wish to go back and work on another.

3   It may also be helpful to use other reminders to reinforce the trigger words and the associated concentration focus – a crib card on the mirror or fridge at home, in the changing room, even on a plaster on the hand in practice. Help your performer to create a crib card for his/her next competition using one of the selected concentration cues.

Programme Three: Improving Concentration by Reducing Anxiety

AIM

To help performers reduce and control anxiety to improve concentration.

Anxiety tends to have a negative effect on concentration – often referred to as choking. It is important therefore to help performers change their perception of high arousal from a negative to a positive experience. This can be achieved either by reducing the level of uncertainty and the importance of the outcome, or by using stress management skills. Before embarking on this programme, ensure you have read the section on controlling anxiety in Chapter Two (page 32).

By the end of this programme, you should be able to improve concentration in potentially stressful situations by helping your performers to:

- change their perception of high arousal
- recognise the negative effects of anxiety on their ability to concentrate
- control anxiety by finding ways to reduce uncertainty, focus on process or performance rather than outcome (especially during competitions) and use relaxation skills to reduce anxiety in training and competition.

In this programme, you will need to work with your performers on one occasion outside coaching for between one and two hours (NB If Step 5 is used, it might be better carried out in a separate session).

❏   Ask your performer to identify the physical and mental symptoms experienced when feeling anxious prior to a competition and to explain its effect on performance. Two examples are offered in case you need prompts:

Symptoms of Mental or Physical Anxiety	Effect on Performance; Friend or Foe?
Why am I putting myself under pressure again, what am I doing here (mental)?	*Negative effect – lots of negative doubts floating round my head*
Butterflies/feelings of nausea (physical)	*Positive effect – looking forward to the competition, know I am ready to perform well*

Discuss the answers together and if necessary, help the performer to understand that high arousal (a level of activation) may constitute readiness to perform optimally (a friend) rather than always anxiety about the forthcoming performance (an enemy). This should give you an insight both into the performer's perceptions, the possible need for relaxation training and whether to focus on reducing physical (somatic) anxiety, mental (cognitive) anxiety or perhaps both.

❏   Alternatively you might assess the performer's perception of the effect of high arousal on performance by chatting through the following questions:

1   What did it feel like just before the competition? Can you remember how your body felt?

2   What did you think about this?

3   Do you remember any other thoughts that were going through your head?

4   Did you feel and think the same before your last high pressure event?

5   Did you feel these thoughts and feelings were good or bad?

You might be able to record their feelings and thoughts in a table in exactly the same way.

3   To reduce anxiety, you may wish to review the way goals are set for competitions. Process and performance goals are more likely to improve concentration, while an overemphasis on outcome goals will probably increase the anxiety – expectations are raised and the focus shifts onto factors that cannot be fully controlled. If process goals are appropriately set and achieved, it is likely the outcome goals will take care of themselves. Select appropriate exercises from Programme Four.

4   You might like to work on thought stopping – particularly if your performer is prone to negative thinking. It may help raise their awareness of negative thinking to encourage them to record all negative thoughts over a week – in training, competition and life in general. Having become aware of the sort of negative thoughts that prevail, you can then help the performer to generate positive statements to replace or counter them. It is important to let the performers generate their own statements – they must own them. Specific programmes on thought stopping can be found in the complementary packs on **Handling Pressure** and **Building Self-confidence.**

5   If you decide to introduce relaxation techniques to your performer, you may wish to encourage your performer to use the script for progressive muscular relaxation[1]. NB This might be better carried out in a separate session.

Alternatively, you may wish to try other techniques such as centring. Some instructions for this were provided in Chapter Two (page 32) but there is more detailed help in the complementary pack **Handling Pressure.**

NB Always remember to review the relaxation training experience with your performer.

---

1   If you decide you need to use relaxation techniques, you are recommended to follow the guidelines offered in the complementary pack, **Handling Pressure**, available from Coachwise 1st4sport (0113-201 5555).

Progressive muscular relaxation

1   First read the following instructions and then choose a quiet place to work through them practically.

2   Instructions:

- Lie down and relax your entire body. If you hear noises, don't try to block them out but focus on your breathing – inhaling, then exhaling slowly. If you want to move slightly, that's OK. Close your eyes, take it easy and relax.

- Tense the muscles of your right lower leg and foot by pointing your toe.

- Hold the tension for 5–6 seconds and then relax. You should be able to feel the tension in the foot and the calf and then totally relax. When you relax, feel the warmth in the muscles. Repeat this procedure again on the right leg and then repeat it twice for the left leg.

- After tensing and relaxing the lower leg and foot, tense (for five seconds) and relax the thigh and buttocks region (twice for each leg). Tense the buttocks and thighs by pushing down with your buttocks.

- Tense and relax the forearm and hand by making a fist. Do this twice for each arm.

- Tense and relax the bicep of each arm by bending at the elbow and pretending you are doing a chin up. Repeat twice for each arm.

- Tense (for five seconds) and relax the back muscles by arching the back up. Tense and relax the back twice.

- Tense the stomach and chest muscles by breathing in and releasing – relaxing. Do this twice.

- Tense the neck and shoulders by shrugging your shoulders (pulling them together) and then releasing them and relaxing.

- Tense the face and forehead by gritting your teeth and pulling your eyebrows together, then relax. Do this twice.

- Mentally scan your body for any tension and release it. Focus on the relaxed feelings in your muscles, and the calming thoughts of your mind set.

After you have worked through this exercise, slowly flex, stretch, inhale and open your eyes before you sit up. Take time to evaluate your ability to relax during this exercise.

Programme Four: Learning to Focus on the Controllable Factors in Performance

AIM

To help performers improve concentration by focusing on factors they can control and learning to use process goals.

To maintain focus on the fundamental cues essential to optimal performance, performers need to concentrate on the controllable factors in the present, the here and now, rather than allowing their concentration to drift back, project forward to the outcome or dwell on factors beyond their control. They therefore need to adopt a process orientation (rather than an outcome orientation) – focus on a process goal – for this reduces anxiety and retains a feeling of control.

Before embarking on this programme, ensure you are familiar with the principles of objective goal-setting, have completed the performer profile in Programme One and read the relevant sections on controlling the controllable in Chapter Two (page 38).

By the end of this programme you should be able to help performers to improve concentration in training and competition by:

- identifying what is and what is not controllable
- setting appropriate process goals around controllable factors for training and competition
- identifying strategies to reach the process goals.

In this programme, you will need to work with your performers on two separate occasions outside coaching – each for between one and two hours, followed by regular work within training sessions and then competitions.

Phase A: Outside coaching session (one hour) to establish with your performer what is and what is not controllable

❏ Ask your performer to list all the factors that affects his/her performance in training/coaching sessions and in competition. Make a list ensuring the performer considers the influential factors outside the sports arena such as school/work, influence of family and other lifestyle factors if appropriate.

NB This will not be a definitive list and may well differ from athlete to athlete and, even with each athlete, change over time.

Next ask the performer to identify all the ones over which:

* he/she currently exercises complete control (eg effort put into training)
* the performer has insufficient control at present (eg temper)
* can never be controlled (eg weather).

Factors Influencing Performance	Can Control	Cannot Currently Control	Impossible to Control

Carefully question if you disagree with the differentiation – you may have misinterpreted the factor. However, accept there may be some currently outside the performer's control (eg food provided at home) that might with renewed strategies be brought more under control. Together try to agree the final list.

Point out the futility in worrying about the factors that are impossible to control – they are usually the same for everyone so nothing can be gained by giving them time and attention. Emphasise the importance of focusing on the factors that it is possible to control – the performer's own technique, the decisions he/she makes, the effort put in, food eaten.

2   Each of the factors identified as controllable but not thought to be under your control, need to be systematically broken down into strategies which will bring that variable under control. With your performer, select one or two factors you feel are outside your control at the moment but that could be brought under greater control. Select the more important and then try to identify a strategy that would help to bring it under greater control.

Factor Currently Outside **my Control** that I Would Like to Bring Under My Control	Strategies for **Controlling** that Factor
Who I listen to before a competition.	• *Identify people who say negative things I do not wish to hear.* • *Identify people who say positive things or with whom I feel at ease before the competition.* • *Only talk to positive people.*
Goal:	

To help develop a professional attitude, work with just one factor at any one time. Turn the strategy into action by agreeing a goal – ensure it is SMARTER – specific, measurable, agreed, realistic, time-framed, exciting and recorded. Do not expect immediate results. Mental and physical control skills take time to acquire. However, by being persistent in your endeavours, results will come. The long-term aim should be to score ten out of ten on every controllable factor.

Phase B: Adopting a process orientation (allow one hour outside coaching session followed by work within a number of training sessions, followed by competitions)

Having grasped the difference between what can and cannot be controlled and set up a programme to start working on these, the performer may now be ready to recognise the importance of using process goals (especially during competition). With your performer, sit down and map out the next phase of training and competition – perhaps over the next three months – and set some longer-term realistic but challenging outcome goals.

Break these down into progressive process goals – it may help to identify positive behaviours that you are both seeking and set process goals to achieve these for both training and competition. Ensure your process goals are always positive and SMARTER, keep them challenging, dynamic and change them as necessary.

Display your goals – it helps commitment and prompts evaluation. If necessary, use prompts in training sessions and competitions (eg display crib cards, place reminders on plasters stuck to the performer's hand) and ask questions about the process goals set during training sessions.

Type of Goal and Time-frame	Specific Goal	Progress Monitoring
Outcome goal for next ....months:		
Process goal/s for:		
Process goal/s for:		
Process goal/s for:		
Process goal/s for:		

Make time regularly to meet to discuss progress against each goal, reset as necessary but ensure goals in competition remain as process goals.

2   With your performer, identify one (or two) process goals for the next training session. Discuss exactly how this can be achieved and design the session appropriately. If necessary, agree how prompts will be used and ensure there is time following the session to feedback and assess whether or not the goal has been achieved. You may wish to record the information in a form similar to the following:

Process goal for session on:		
Training Session		**Reminders**
Introduction:		
Main Session:		
Conclusion:		
Evaluation:		
Goal Achieved/ Not Achieved (give reasons):		
Action Plan:		

You will need to work on the use of process goals very frequently in order to change the performer's orientation away from outcome towards process goals. As and when the performer is ready, start to set and monitor process goals in competition. Keep working on controlling the controllables through the setting of process goals.

Programme Five: Developing Routines to Improve Concentration

AIM

To help performers develop routines for focusing and refocusing.

One way to minimise distraction and focus concentration is to develop a routine – not just prior to the competition but whenever there is a break in action or a situation to focus or refocus attention onto the relevant concentration cues. They can help performers to:

• concentrate on the performance process more effectively

• control thought processes and avoid over-analysis

• adopt a more consistent approach to performance, both mentally and physically

• increase feelings of control which can boost self-confidence.

Ensure you have read the relevant section in Chapter Two on routines (page 44) before embarking on this programme with your performer. By the end of this programme, you should be able to help performers to:

• determine when routines will be beneficial to them

• identify and implement a pre-competition routine

• identify and implement a refocusing routine.

NB There is no logical progression between Phase A and B so you can choose which to do first. Each requires one session outside coaching and then regular practice time in training sessions and ultimately competitions.

Phase A: Developing a refocusing performance routine (allow one hour outside coaching session time, regular practice time in training sessions for several weeks, then inclusion in competitions)

1   With your performers, identify opportunities in competition when performance routines might be used to focus or refocus attention. Then together determine where attention should be placed.

NB If the performer already uses a routine, this might be a useful place to start:

Specific Situations when Routines might be Used to Focus or Refocus	Appropriate Focus of Attention

2   Select one situation that requires a focusing routine – it may help to select a positive situation first (eg taking a line-out throw in rugby, preparing to vault in gymnastics) rather than the more complex refocusing routines needed to overcome emotional reactions (eg giving away a penalty in rugby, falling off the beam in gymnastics). Remember it needs to be quick and easy to execute. You may wish to adjust the breathe-focus-act example suggested on page 52.

Routine for: (name)		For: (situation)	

2   Next you need to ask your performers to practise the routine or specific elements of it before all practice and training sessions. It should be made clear that the routine can be changed and refined until the performer is happy with both the components and the timing of the programme. When time allows prior to training sessions, the performer should complete all the elements of the routine. You may wish to video the routine and then discuss various elements more fully with the performer.

3   Once confident, the programme can be tested before minor competitions and then finally before important competitions. Remember your performers will have more confidence in their routines if its effectiveness is monitored. This might be done by you – perhaps with the use of a check-list or video.

Check that:

- each element of the routine is still needed (some aspect may have been altered or should be altered)

- the routine is carried out according to the check-list (eg component actions, sequence, timing)

- the routine has not become a prop that would create anxiety if for some reason it could not be used (ie its use was dependent on factors that cannot always be controlled).

4   Once the pre-competition routine is working effectively, it may be advisable to work out some contingency routine adjustments. You might conduct a *what if* session with your performer/s. First brainstorm on anything (controllable or not) that could prevent the routine from being fully executed (eg limited facility at the venue, lack of time). Then work systematically through the list and together determine the best course of action for each eventuality. You may then find it necessary either to add one or two planning steps to the routine (eg checking more fully on details of the facility prior to the competition) to control the controllables or to practise an amended routine for coping with the uncontrollable situations. Always build from practice sessions to simulated situations to minor competitions and monitor its effectiveness.

Programme Six: Using Imagery to Improve Concentration

AIM

To help performers use imagery to improve concentration.

Imagery is a very flexible mental skill that can be used in a number of ways – improving concentration is just one of them. For example, it can be used to:

- promote relaxation and reduce anxiety, thereby improving focus
- rehearse performing well in high pressure situations which have proved very distracting – reinforcing the link between attention on relevant concentration cues and the ensuing successful performance (Programme Two)
- rehearse the use of refocusing routines and pre-competition routines (Programme Five).

By the end of this programme, you should be able to:

- assess your performer's ability to use imagery
- identify where imagery skills might be incorporated into other techniques to assist concentration.

In this programme, you will need to work with your performers on two separate occasions outside coaching – each for between one and two hours.

Phase A: Assessing imagery skills (allow one hour outside coaching session time)

Although the introduction and development of imagery skills is beyond the scope of this pack; one exercise is provided for you to use with your performers – it may offer a means of assessing their ability to use this skill. In as relaxed an environment as possible (you may wish to start with the exercise in Programme Six), read the following script to your performers, allowing plenty of time for them to focus on each stimulus – as much as 5–10 seconds between each statement to let the performer build up the image.:

See yourself picking up an orange from a fruit bowl. Note the colours of the rest of the fruit in the bowl. The yellow of the bananas, the green and red of the apples, the black of the grapes and the orange of the oranges and satsumas. Feel the surface of the orange in your fingers and note its smell. (See the zest spring from the orange). Dig your fingernails into the skin. and as you continue to peel the skin away, be aware of the smell of the orange. Note the noise as you peel the orange, and split the orange into segments. Feel the sticky zest and juice on your fingers. Experience the taste of the orange, and the feel in your mouth and on your teeth as you bite into a segment and chew it.

If the performer has no experience of using imagery and particularly if he/she had difficulty with this exercise, you will need to transfer onto some imagery training work before pursuing this programme. The sorts of questions you should be able to answer include:

- How easily is your performer able to use imagery?
- Which senses does he/she prefer?
- Does he/she use internal or external perspectives (visualisation)?
- How can I modify training to encourage the use of imagery?
- Does my performer set goals for imagery practice?
- Does he/she evaluate the effectiveness of the imagery?

Phase B: Incorporating imagery into other strategies to improve concentration (allow one hour outside coaching sessions per session)

1 Review with your performer an appropriate concentration cue for a well learnt technique. Using a simple breathing control strategy to help relaxation, ask your performer to image the execution of the technique ensuring the correct focus.

NB It may be appropriate for you as the coach to prepare a script of the imagery session that you wish to practise (see Phase A in this programme).

This activity can and should be repeated systematically. The technique highlighted may progress from a well learnt skill to a new technique, from performance in training to performance in more and more important competitions and from a closed skill (with very little variability) to an open skill (where many variables may change).

2 Select with your performer a specific routine (pre-competition or refocusing routines). Using a simple breathing control strategy to help relaxation, ask your performer to visualise the routine or part of the routine. Again, it may be appropriate to construct a script for initial use in this activity.

If it is a pre-competition routine, encourage the performer to imagine arriving at the venue and then rehearsing each step (or a specified step) of the routine. Emphasis should be placed on seeing him/herself in the IPS, in an appropriate state of readiness, in control and with the appropriate focus – ready to start the competition.

If it is a refocusing routine, encourage the performer to visualise the situation in as much detail as possible – the preceding few seconds before the stoppage, using the trigger, word, action or image and seeing him/herself going through the routine successfully and ready to restart in a positive and focused frame of mind.

As imagery skills improve, they can be used to help develop and practise routines in emotive situations – such as after errors or distracting situations. Encourage them to visualise the situation but this time make the correct or successful decision rather than a mistake. As the performer gains experience and skill, this type of practice can be completed with the coach providing extra distractions (eg an audiotape containing distracting sounds such as crowd noises), or perhaps when the performer is not active during a training session (on the bench, between sets) so the training session or other performers can provide the distraction.

NB This may be much more effective if you write an individualised imagery script.

Programme Seven: Employing Distraction Training

AIM

To devise simulation exercises to help performers deal with distractions.

Simulations are really like dress rehearsals and in many of the preceding programmes, you have already been encouraged to use them as you move strategies developed in training into the competitive situation. The emphasis in this programme is to identify and simulate particular distractions to test the performer's ability to put into practice effectively some of the strategies he/she has been trying to learn to improve concentration. Coaches need to be creative but realistic in the way they set up simulated situations – ones that place more and more pressure on the performer, so creating the sort of anxiety-evoking situations that threaten concentration in competitions.

Before embarking on this programme, ensure you have read Section 2.7 (page 60) and that your performer has already some well-developed strategies for dealing with distractions (any of those introduced in Programmes Two to Five). By the end of this programme, you should be able to:

- devise simulation exercises
- assess your performer's ability to cope with distractions.

In this programme, you will need to work with your performers for about one hour outside coaching sessions. You will then need to set up specific training sessions for simulated work.

First you need to identify with your performers the factors that cause concentration problems. Some of these may already have been elicited indirectly if you have already worked through Phase A of Programme Four. Make a list of the sort of distractions that most frequently interfere with your performer's ability to maintain focus or refocus.

Distractions:

-
-
-
-
-

Check if there is a pattern or common stimulus causing the problem. Ask yourself whether it is from a controllable or uncontrollable source, is it triggered by a particular emotion (eg anxiety, frustration) or is it caused by information overload and insufficient time to make decisions about action? Any of these situations can be replicated in training with a little care and creativity.

2   Select a distraction and devise a simulated situation in which you can evoke in training the stimulus for the distraction to occur. Take time to plan this for it must be as sport-specific, realistic and safe as possible and it may be difficult to repeat the exercise without destroying reality. Ensure your performer has the necessary strategies to cope before implementing it and assessing the performer's ability to ignore the distraction or successfully implement a refocusing strategy.

Strategy:

-
-
-
-
-

3   Put the plan into action and evaluate the outcome. Ensure there is sufficient time after the session to debrief the performer fully and action plan as necessary. Ensure you finish on a positive note.

Programme Eight: Improving Concentration through the Use of Mental Skills

AIM

To integrate mental skills for improving concentration into your performers' training programmes.

In the preceding sections you identified your performer's strengths and weaknesses and tried a number of mental skills and strategies to improve concentration. However, this is just the beginning. Concentration must be nurtured constantly and the mental skills your performer has begun to develop need to be used appropriately throughout training and competition programmes.

By the end of this programme, you should be able to:

- identify with each performer the best strategies to develop his/her concentration
- determine how these strategies and mental skills will be integrated into training programmes
- plan, conduct and evaluate the mental skills components of a series of coaching sessions
- evaluate progress using the profiling technique used in Programme One.

In this final programme, you will need to work with your performers for about one hour outside coaching sessions, then work for an extended period of time in coaching sessions and competitions. Finally you will need a one hour profiling session to evaluate progress.

Phase A: Work with your performer for 1–2 hours outside normal coaching sessions.

Sit down with your performer and use profiling techniques to discuss the following questions:

- How would you now rate your concentration skills? Refer back to the performance profile and use the ten point rating score. From this, determine with your performer the importance of further work on concentration.

- Determine which mental skills and strategies the performer has found most helpful in gaining or maintaining concentration – identifying concentration cues, employing process goals and working to control the controllables, developing refocusing and pre-competition routines, using imagery or distraction training. Write in the skills/strategy and score each on the profile.

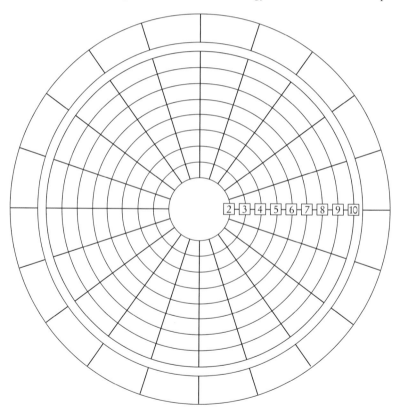

- Ask your performer to what extent he/she likes to use each skill (having had a chance to practise each) and mark this on the profile in another colour.

2   From this, draw up an action plan with your performer about which skills to develop further, the strategy to be used, when in the training programme this should be done and what sort of realistic goal might be set over what time-frame. This obviously needs to fit in with other priorities over the next three or six months. Then you need to break this down into a number of shorter-term process goals that can be set over a number of training sessions and then competitions.

Long-term outcome goal regarding concentration work over the next .... months.	
Shorter-term process goals to implement in .... competition on .... NB You will need several of these.	
Shorter-term process goal to implement in a simulated competitive situation in	
Shorter-term process goals to implement in .... training sessions during week beginning .... NB You will need several of these.	
Shorter-term process goals to implement at home during week beginning .... NB You may need more than one of these.	

Some examples are provided in the following table:

Longer-term Goal:	Develop use of key/trigger words to initiate refocusing routine to use at every stoppage in the game to improve focus. **By end of May**
Short-term Goal:	With performer, identify suitable trigger words and use in all training sessions. **Throughout January**
Short-term Goal:	Use trigger word and routine in all non-league matches. **Early February**
Short-term Goal:	Use trigger word and routine in all matches. **February/March**
Short-term Goal:	Use trigger word and routine in play-offs at the end of the season. **March**

Phase B: Over an extended period (for example three months) of coaching sessions and competitions, followed by a one hour session outside coaching.

1 You will then need to put these plans into practice over a series of coaching sessions and competitions and monitor progress against the goals carefully.

2 After an appropriate period of time (determined by your goal-setting exercise), you should return to Step 8 in the profiling exercises in Programme One to assess progress.

Final Summary

Using mental skills is not a quick fix to improving concentration. Their use will only be effective if the skills are regularly practised and time is built into the programme to monitor and adapt their use. As your performers develop, they will build up a menu of mental skills. Like all aspects of performance preparation, you and your performers should emphasise different skills as and when required.

Coaches will need to provide the necessary support and guidance to help performers develop, practise and hone their mental skills. The amount of help and support will vary. However, ultimately it is the performer who must take responsibility for the development and use of mental skills and strategies, in the same way they must be encouraged and empowered to take responsibility for every aspect of performance.

Recommended further reading

Bull, S.J. (1991) **Sport Psychology: A Self-help Guide.** Marlborough: Crowood Press. ISBN 1-85223-568-3

Butler, R. (1996) **Performance Profiling.** Leeds: Coachwise Solutions/The National Coaching Foundation. ISBN 0-947850-36-8

Hardy, L. Jones, G. and Gould, D. (1996) **Understanding Psychological Preparation for Sport: Theory and Practice.** Chichester: Wiley. ISBN 0-471-95787-9

Loudis, L. Lobitz, C. and Singer, K. (1988) 'Constructive thinking: changing your self talk'. In Loudis, L. **Skiing Out of Your Mind**. Huddersfield: Springfield Books Ltd. ISBN 0-947655-42-5

Mace, R. (2002) **With Sport in Mind: An Introduction to Mental Skills Training.** Droitwich Spa: Sport in Mind Ltd. ISBN 0-9535457-3-9

Morris, T. (1997) **Psychological Skills Training in Sport.** Leeds, Coachwise Solutions/The National Coaching Foundation. ISBN 0-947850-78-3

Sellars, C. (1997) **Building Self-confidence.** Leeds, Coachwise Solutions/The National Coaching Foundation. ISBN 0-947850-11-2